PRAISE FOR *Better Than College*

"Before you spend four years in college, devote four hours to hearing what Blake has to say."
—Seth Godin, author of *Stop Stealing Dreams*

"Higher education in America is on the brink of disruption. As prices rise and relevance declines, a chorus of voices is urging us to rethink college as we know it. And few of those voices are clearer or more compelling than Blake Boles. *Better Than College* is a clarion call for independent thinkers and self-directed young people to take control of their learning. Bypassing college may not be the right move for everyone, but reading this book will help anyone think anew about education and the future."
—Daniel H. Pink, author of *Drive* and *A Whole New Mind*

"The possibilities for success without college are rich and glorious—and potentially so confusing in their vastness as to be crippling. Blake Boles offers a clear and compelling roadmap: grounded in real-life examples and insightful analysis, lofted by a wide and exuberant sense of what life can become. *Better Than College* is perfectly tailored for its intended audience—youth on the threshold of adulthood. It will also, however, be a wonderful resource for adults who yearn to bring their work into alignment with their passions, and for families who want their children to grow toward successful and joyful careers."
—Grace Llewellyn, author of
The Teenage Liberation Handbook

"A brilliant and important proposal. The unquestioned college path deserves to be challenged, and this is the right book to do it."
—Derek Sivers, founder of CD Baby, sivers.org

"How did we get tricked into believing that success, fortune, and self-knowledge only come with a college degree? *Better Than College* explodes this myth and shows how any young adult can craft a powerful and affordable higher education—no institution required."

—Michael Ellsberg, author of *The Education of Millionaires*

"*Better Than College* gives the tools, and just as important, the encouragement self-learners need to explore all their options."

—Anya Kamenetz, author of *DIY U* and
The Edupunks' Guide to a DIY Credential

"Blake Boles has scouted out information and ideas useful to more than just young adults. He has outlined options and filled in details for people of any age who want to see paths to learning and living outside of traditional schools. There is joy and hope in new directions, and Blake is an inspirational guide."

—Sandra Dodd, author of *The Big Book of Unschooling*

"Blake convincingly argues that not everyone benefits from a traditional college education, and he presents a highly researched guide for pursuing self-directed education. This is a practical manual for motivated students on how to take your education into your own hands and thrive in the new world of work."

—Ben Casnocha, coauthor of *The Start-Up of You: Adapt to the Future, Invest in Yourself, and Transform Your Career*

"Unsure about college? Blake Boles has written a clear and wildly inspirational guide for those who long for a meaningful way to gain self-knowledge, acquire relevant experience and dive into full engagement. This isn't a second-best proposition for young people 'just not cut out for college'—it's a bold blueprint for anyone looking to become focused, fired up and ready to define and follow their own successful path."

—Maya Frost, author of *The New Global Student: Skip the SAT, Save Thousands on Tuition and Get a Truly International Education*

"If you are ready to take control of your learning—and save a bundle of money at the same time—this book will provide you with compelling inspiration and practical information. You couldn't choose a better guide to creating your own future."

—Wendy Priesnitz, editor of *Life Learning Magazine* and author of *Beyond School: Living As If School Doesn't Exist*

"It's very easy for a young person today to walk straight from high school into college and emerge four years later, deep into their twenties, with almost no experience running their own lives, no practical knowledge or skills, and the belief that they have to be institutionally instructed to learn anything. And carrying a giant load of debt too! Are you sure that four-year degree is as valuable and indispensable as you hope it is? Now more than ever is the time to look closely at the possibilities, think hard and carefully, and not just fall into decisions. There are lots of reasons to go to college, and lots of reasons not to, and either way *Better Than College* is a tremendous place to start: the writing is straightforward, nondogmatic, and honest. If you're planning to go (or return) to college (or not), read this book first!"

—Matt Hern, founder of the Purple Thistle Centre and author of *Field Day* and *Everywhere All the Time*

"*Better Than College* powerfully demonstrates our cultural misconception that a college degree is the only ticket to a higher education and a successful life."

—Diane Flynn Keith, editor of Homefires.com

"More and more young adults are realizing that college has little to offer them other than wasted time and debt. Unfortunately, most of society doesn't get it, because most of society has been conditioned to believe the lie that college is the only path to professional success and financial security. Blake Boles provides these young adults with a roadmap (and three questions that all young adults should ask themselves) that will help guide them toward more meaningful experiences, and the ammunition they need to deal with the naysayers."

—Antonio Buehler, founder of Buehler Education

"During my 51 years and continuing work in education, I've read hundreds of books on education and found exactly three of them to be compelling, completely engaging, and highly inspirational. *Better Than College* is one of these three. If you have any thoughts about going to college—even if you're committed to obtaining a college degree—read *Better Than College*; it will prompt deep thinking about your life direction."

—Wes Beach, author of *Forging Paths* and director of Beach High School

Better Than College

BETTER THAN COLLEGE

HOW TO BUILD A SUCCESSFUL LIFE WITHOUT A FOUR-YEAR DEGREE

BLAKE BOLES

TELLS PEAK PRESS

Published in the United States by Tells Peak Press, Loon Lake, CA.

http://www.tellspeak.com

While the author has made every effort to provide accurate Internet addresses at the time of publication, neither the publisher nor the author assumes any responsibility for errors, or for changes that occur after publication. Further, the publisher does not have any control over and does not assume any responsibility for third-party websites or their content.

Publisher's Cataloging-In-Publication Data

Boles, Blake.
    Better than college : how to build a successful life without a four-year degree / Blake Boles. — 1st ed.
        p. : ill. ; cm.
    Includes bibliographical references and index.
    ISBN: 978-0-9860119-0-0
    1. Self-culture. 2. Alternative education. 3. Education, Higher.
4. Success. I. Title.
LC32.B65 2012
371.3943   2012938461

Kindle ISBN: 978-0-9860119-1-7
ePub ISBN: 978-0-9860119-2-4

Book design by Eric Butler
Cover design by Kristen Haff

10 9 8 7 6 5 4 3 2 1

First Edition

DEDICATED TO:

The brilliant, courageous, and inspirational teenagers of
Not Back to School Camp, Deer Crossing Camp,
and Unschool Adventures

CONTENTS

PREFACE

A few notes on terminology:

- The word "college" in this book refers to four-year colleges and universities that lead to a bachelor of arts (BA) or bachelor of science (BS) degree.

- The phrase "Zero Tuition College" (ZTC) designates the method of self-directed learning described in this book.

- The ZTC online community may be found at www.ztcollege.com.

Does This Book Deserve Your Time?

Thank you for giving this book a chance. I realize that my thesis—that you can skip four-year college and still get a higher education—may seem nuts. But spend a few moments considering the propositions below, and you'll begin to see why Zero Tuition College, the alternative learning method described in this book, holds just as much life-changing potential as traditional college.

Proposition #1: College is just too expensive.

Today, the liberal arts college experience offers many valuable things: exposure to new ideas, analytical skills, social networks, support, accountability, and the opportunity to live independently. But these good things come at a high price. The average family will shell out roughly $20,000 per year for tuition and living expenses,[1] while the average student who takes out loans will graduate with more than $25,000 of debt.[2]

---

1 "Average Undergraduate Tuition and Fees and Room and Board Rates," National Center for Education Statistics, prepared October 2010, http://nces.ed.gov/programs/digest/d10/tables/dt10_345.asp.

2 Blake Ellis, "Average Student Loan Debt Tops $25,000," *CNN Money*, November 3, 2011, http://money.cnn.com/2011/11/03/pf/student_loan_debt/index.htm.

And this isn't a recent trend: since the 1950s, college tuition has risen almost twice as fast as inflation.[3]

When the price of oil rises, we look more seriously at alternative energy. When a business raises its prices, we consider different ways that we could obtain the same goods or services. But even though the price of college has skyrocketed, we flood its gates. Why?

Proposition #2: Higher education and college are not the same thing.

We spend big bucks on college because we've confused receiving a college degree with getting a higher education. They're two different things.

A college degree proves that you can survive four years at an institution. It's a piece of paper that says, "I followed a prescribed path to success."

A higher education, though, is first and foremost the capacity to self-direct your life. Someone who has a higher education can define her own vision of success and pursue it, even in the face of difficulty.

College is one path to a higher education, but it's not the only one. Sometimes college graduates lead self-directed lives, but sometimes they don't; a college degree does not guarantee a higher education.

---

3   "Tuition Inflation," The Smart Student Guide to Financial Aid, accessed October 14, 2010, http://www.finaid.org/savings/tuition-inflation.phtml.

Proposition #3: You can give yourself a higher education without college.

So how do you give yourself a higher education, if not via college? That's the challenge this book addresses. Here's an overview of the answer:

Instead of following someone else's curriculum, self-directed learners begin by asking themselves what fascinates and drives them. Their journey begins—and ends—with self-knowledge.

Instead of taking full-time classes, self-directed learners give themselves assignments that they find interesting, eye-opening, and challenging. They start businesses, find internships, travel the world, read and write about things that fascinate them, and work for organizations they admire. Many college students do these things too, but the difference is that self-directed learners don't wait for anyone's permission to begin learning.

Instead of working on homework, papers, and presentations destined to be seen once and tossed into a trash can, self-directed learners turn much of their hard work into useful products for other people. They write blogs, build startups, create art, record videos, teach their skills, and sell their services. They keep an eye out for the innumerable ways that they can improve someone else's life.

Instead of relying mainly upon professors and college guidance counselors to help direct their educational process, self-directed learners seek the mentorship of a variety of accomplished individuals. They consult family, friends, businesspeople, writers, researchers, working professionals, retirees, or anyone else who might help them. They keep themselves accountable by sharing their goals publicly and asking friends and mentors to keep them on track.

Instead of purchasing peer community through college, self-directed learners meet friends through their work, hobbies, travel, networking, and social media—just as people do in the real world. They try to surround themselves with as many smart people as they can.

To become financially secure, self-directed learners figure out how to market themselves, get hired in unconventional ways, start their own ventures, and live within their means. They recognize that these abilities—not a degree—are the true assets of an economically resilient life.

By doing these things, self-directed learners gain many of the benefits that we associate with higher education—knowledge, skills, self-awareness, exposure, emotional growth, self-discipline, and work opportunities—for a radically lower price than the tuition of a traditional college.

Proposition #4: Skipping college isn't the best idea for everyone.

Replacing college with self-directed learning is a good idea for many students, but not everyone. There are some people for whom college is clearly the best choice.

If your goal is to enter a licensed profession—to become a doctor, lawyer, architect, public school teacher, engineer, or other government-licensed professional—then you have a good reason to go to college.

If you want to do PhD-level work—to study cancer, publish neuroscience papers, or teach university-level history—then you have a good reason to go to college.[4]

If you'd like to work for a major investment bank, consulting firm, or other wealthy institution that heavily values adherence to social norms, then you have a good reason to go to college.

If you crave the challenge of reading (and writing) dense academic content and want to work with specific professors, then you have a good reason to go to college.

But if, on the other hand:

- you suspect that becoming a doctor, lawyer, architect, scientist, professor, or financier is really somebody else's goal for you;

---

4 Technically, you just need a graduate degree to enter most licensed professions or do PhD-level work. And not all graduate programs require an undergraduate degree.

- you're loosely interested in the liberal arts, studio art, technology, entrepreneurship, or working with your hands;

- you suspect that you haven't seen enough of the world to really focus in college;

- you're mostly interested in the social aspect of college; or

- you're simply unsure about everything,

then postponing, leaving, or skipping college might be the best thing you ever do.

Proposition #5: It's a gamble either way.

If you skip or leave college in order to pursue a self-directed, adventurous, and entrepreneurial higher education, you're taking a gamble. It might not work out. You may live with your parents for a while, have trouble making money, and suffer the embarrassment of trying something different and failing. You may have to go back to school.

But if you go to college because you believe it's a safe path, because you want to avoid criticism, or even for one of the aforementioned good reasons, you're also taking a gamble.

It might not work out. You may live with your parents for a while and have trouble making money. You may have to go back to school. But—unlike in the self-directed path—you may end up with massive amounts of student loan debt at the time in your life when you're supposed to be most free.

I'm not able to tell you which gamble is more appropriate for you. But I'm confident that the first gamble—crafting your own adventurous and entrepreneurial higher education—will teach you things about yourself that the second never could.

Proposition #6: There's a culture of fear around college, but it's the wrong fear.

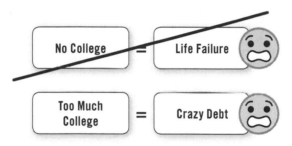

It's difficult to make a rational decision about college when parents, politicians, educators, and pretty much everyone else rallies behind a college-for-all banner. When you choose to skip college to pursue your own higher education, you're truly bucking the establishment. That's a scary thing to do.

To illustrate: when I started writing articles about ZTC, my friend Sarah wrote me an e-mail.

"There is a cultural voice that lives inside my head," Sarah explained. "Whenever I start reading an article that's critical of college, this voice starts shouting, *You need a college degree to be taken seriously and earn a real living!* It takes a lot of work to quiet that voice down. Perhaps you can launch a preemptive strike against it?"

That's when I realized that this book needed to be written. We're in the midst of a college mania that threatens the livelihoods of indebted students as well as the financial stability of the countries that provide billions of dollars in easy loans to those students.

At the time of writing, total outstanding student loan debt in the US had reached one trillion dollars—roughly equal to the amount of credit card debt.[5] But, unlike credit card debt, student loan debt survives bankruptcy. Short of fleeing the country, you can't escape your student loans.[6]

This is the real culture of fear that should surround college: not that purposefully skipping college will ruin your life, but that mindlessly attending college (or graduate school) may lock you into a huge pile of debt from which you can never escape.

---

5   Eyder Peralta, "Americans' Student Loan Balance Now Exceeds $1 Trillion," *The Two-Way: NPR's News Blog*, October 19, 2011, http://www.npr.org/ blogs/thetwo-way/2011/10/19/141512824/americans-student-loan-balance-now-exceeds-1-trillion.

6   Why? Because the collateral for a student loan is the student's brain. When a housing market collapses, a lender can reclaim a house. But when a student defaults on his loan, a lender can't reclaim the knowledge locked inside the student's brain. Or, as my friend R. Brent Mattis explains it:

"Imagine you were the loan officer at a bank. A budding entrepreneur comes into your office and says, 'Hi, I'd like to borrow $100,000 to start a business.'

"You say, 'Great, what can you pledge as collateral for the loan?'

"He says, 'Nothing.'

"So you say, 'How do you plan to use the loan?'

"He says, 'Oh, I don't know. I'll probably spend four years broadening my skill set and learning the attributes necessary to be an excellent businessman.'

"The loan officer's head would probably explode."

To Sarah and everyone else who suffers from the little shouting voice, please consider this book an intercontinental ballistic missile aimed at the heart of the assumption that you need a college degree to be taken seriously and earn a real living. You don't. This book explains why—and shows what to do instead.

My Story

I don't expect you to be a quick convert to the ideas behind Zero Tuition College. I wasn't. Until a few important experiences changed my mind, I thought college was the be-all and end-all of young adulthood. The story starts at my own college, the University of California, Berkeley.

From the day that I stepped onto Berkeley's campus in 2001, college offered salvation from the mind-numbing boredom of high school. Never before had I been surrounded by a community of people who took ideas seriously. Inspired by the mysteries of black holes, dark matter, and the Big Bang, I began as an astrophysics major. But after two years of physics courses and a stint as an undergraduate research assistant, I decided that I wasn't serious enough about science to pursue it as a career.

Around the same time, a friend handed me a book by former New York City schoolteacher John Taylor Gatto, who called into question the basic purpose of education.[7] Reading Gatto's arguments felt like meeting a soul mate, and I realized immediately that I wanted to dedicate myself to alternative education. Forget the distant galaxies—there were bigger mysteries to solve here on earth.

To pursue my new calling, I pestered the UC Berkeley administration until they let me design my own major in alternative education. What followed was a high-energy, self-directed, two-year adventure that changed my life. Given free

---

7   John Taylor Gatto, *A Different Kind of Teacher: Solving the Crisis of American Schooling* (Albany: Berkeley Hill Books, 2000).

rein, I spent my time volunteering at local schools, leading my own undergraduate education course, writing a 40-page thesis, and interviewing pioneers in the field of alternative schooling. No one in the university held my hand; I guided myself, seeking mentorship from friends, family, and new contacts. Two Berkeley professors assisted my thesis efforts but otherwise left me alone. In 2004, I graduated with honors and high hopes, enlivened by the success of my college journey.

After an experience like this, I naturally believed that four-year college ought to be the goal of any ambitious young adult. But shortly after graduating, I began to see that college didn't work as well for everyone else as it did for me. More significantly, I saw that my self-directed higher education might not have required college at all.

First, I saw the problem of student debt. I was lucky enough to attend UC Berkeley for a dirt-cheap annual tuition of $7000, which my family was able to pay outright. Young adults without similar privilege graduated with $20,000 or more in student loans that demanded high-paying careers directly after college. I enjoyed years of low-income/high-value job experiments and adventures after graduating, while many of my debt-strapped peers found themselves locked into full-time jobs. Then the 2008–2009 recession hit, and unemployment skyrocketed as a new wave of graduates struggled to find the high-paying jobs to which they were supposedly entitled. In the meantime, their student loan payments began piling up. College's high price tag, I saw, could close doors as readily as it could open them.

Next, I realized that much of my college success came from Berkeley's unique advantages. Most colleges don't make it easy to escape an unsatisfying major, design your own classes, or do extensive independent study. I wrongly assumed that every State U and ivy-covered private school offered great opportunities for self-directing your education. They don't.

Finally, I realized that my self-directed awakening—the experience that created my most positive associations with college—wasn't a phenomenon unique to college. In fact, there was an entire world of young adults seeking and finding self-directed success: the "unschoolers."

A young adult unschooler is someone who designs his own education instead of following a formal curriculum. In the eyes of the law, unschoolers are officially homeschoolers, but unschooling is a world apart from traditional homeschooling, both philosophically and practically.[8] In my post-college work I met hundreds of teen unschoolers who were traveling the world, building websites, starting businesses, interning, volunteering, reading extensively, and debating serious ideas—all instead of going to school. Many unschoolers went on to college, but many others chose to skip college and continue living their lives as self-directed young adults.[9]

At first I was skeptical of these college-skippers—without college, how could someone possibly have the epiphany that I did? But as I spent more time watching, traveling with, and listening to college-skipping unschoolers, I began to understand. These young adults were doing everything that I did at Berkeley—learning deeply, developing mastery, becoming exposed to new fields, adventuring, building work experience, and following their passions—without the college price tag.

---

8   For a concise introduction to unschooling, visit http://www.holtgws.com/unschooling.html.

9   I documented the process of getting into college as an unschooler in my 2009 book, *College Without High School* (Gabriola: New Society Publishers).

In early 2010 I listened to a 20-year-old unschooler speak about her decision to leave a respected liberal arts school—to which she had a full-ride scholarship—in order to learn on her own. At that moment, I finally discarded my college-for-all belief. No longer would I recommend college to every young person I met. Instead I started asking them—and myself— about the best ways to self-direct a higher education.

Whether you choose to skip college or not, I hope that through ZTC you'll find a bit of timeless wisdom for leading a more self-directed life. I love hearing from readers, and I would be honored if you wrote to me (yourstruly@blakebo-les.com). Also, please explore the online ZTC community at http://www.ztcollege.com, where you can connect with self-directed young people and knowledgeable adults from across the world.

GOOD REASONS TO SKIP COLLEGE

What Could You Do with $20,000?

Imagine that you've been accepted to the college of your dreams, and the school has given you a full-ride scholarship. In celebration, you and your family spend your college savings on home improvements, philanthropic donations, and an extravagant vacation.

But then tragedy strikes. The college calls and says that it's closing. Yet they make you an offer: instead of leaving you in the cold, they'll give you $20,000 per year so you can give yourself a higher education. The catch is that you can't spend it on another college. You've got to do it yourself.

So the question is: what would you do during the nine-month academic year if you were given $20,000 but couldn't go to college?

*   *   *

I've asked hundreds of teens, young adults, and parents across the country to consider this thought experiment. Their replies are consistent:

- I would travel the world.

- I would use it to pay for living expenses so I could intern or volunteer and figure out what I really want to do.

- I would start one or two businesses and not worry about whether they fail.

- I would put it away for the future.

I thought hard about my own answer. If I had $20,000 to spend on my education for a nine-month academic year, I would spend:

- $4500 for six months of living expenses (room, board, and transportation; $750 per month) in a thriving city where I could live with friends or interesting strangers.

- $3000 for 100 hours of private life coaching or instruction in writing, entrepreneurship, sports, music, art, or a foreign language.

- $2500 for a three-month budget backpacking trip through multiple countries (both developed and developing).

- $1500 for new software, a new laptop, or equipment needed for my learning projects.

- $1000 as startup funds for one or two business ventures.

- $1000 for two or three round-trip plane tickets, five long train trips, or one epic road trip to attend conferences, competitions, and big events and to visit family, friends, and mentors across the country.

- $600 for a literary feast: a one-year university library membership and 40 new books.

- $500 for smartphone service (invaluable for self-directed learning on the fly).

- $200 for high-speed internet, which opens the door to Google, TED Talks, YouTube, university webcasts, blogs, podcasts, and everything else on the Internet.

- $100 for one year of website hosting for a blog and portfolio.

- $100 for a pair of athletic shoes for running and pickup sports games.

- $5000 to invest in a mutual fund.

If I followed this budget for four years, adding $5000 to my mutual fund each year (at 4% yield), I could actually end up with a $22,000 nest egg—almost the amount of debt with which the average college student graduates. And that's assuming my business ventures don't work out.

Then there are the activities I could do that would cost nothing:

- Interning, volunteering, or working for an organization that I admire.

- Seeking the mentorship of friends, family, and other trusted people.

- Interviewing, shadowing, or apprenticing with experts in my fields of interest.

- Reflecting, journaling, and meditating.

By focusing on these low-cost and high-value activities, I may not need to spend even $20,000 per year on my higher education. With creativity and resourcefulness, I could spend $10,000 or less per year—a sum readily accessible with a combination of hard work, fundraising, and parental support.[10]

---

10   For advice on funding your Zero Tuition College experience, visit http://www.ztcollege.com.

The Price of Self-Knowledge

Here's another thought experiment:

Imagine you just got accepted to college. It doesn't matter whether it's Stanford or State U—either way, you've passed one of life's great hurdles, and you're on your way to your future.

Now imagine it's four years later, and you've just graduated. Let's assume that you gained a ton of knowledge, connected with intelligent people, and earned a degree, all of which you use to land a well-paid job.

Now it's the first day of work. You're the new kid from MIT/Stanford/Reed/State U/etc. You're on top of the world—and you've got your college education to thank for it.

But then, one day, the honeymoon ends. All of a sudden, no one cares about your degree or connections. Instead, you're being judged on a new set of criteria: Do you take pride in your work? Do you work well with others? Can you show up on time and motivate yourself? Can you teach yourself new skills? Are you actually a good fit for this position, or did you take it based on misguided assumptions?

Just like everyone else in the world, your long-term success hinges upon a set of knowledge and competencies that have little to do with your grade point average, personal connections, or a framed piece of paper. More crucially, your success depends on your self-knowledge.

Self-knowledge is the deep understanding of one's personality, values, strengths, flaws, and work habits that arises from:

- immersing yourself in new lands, workplaces, and cultures;

- exploring new philosophies, spiritual beliefs, and political views;

- striving to understand the questions that fascinate you;

- pushing yourself beyond your comfort zone (and perhaps recruiting someone else to push you too);

- meeting, conversing with, and attempting to understand hundreds of new people; and

- reflecting on your experiences.

Self-knowledge is the skeleton key that unlocks the answers to a number of questions: What are my deepest needs, and how do I fulfill them? In what environment do I work best? Should I work for myself or someone else? How can I improve myself? How can I personally change the world for the better?

People who lack self-knowledge may have a hard time finding satisfying work, gaining genuine respect, or forming deep relationships. People with self-knowledge, on the other hand, can find work, respect, and relationships even in difficult circumstances.

Of course, you can gain self-knowledge in college as well. That's one of the big reasons—stated or unstated—that many people want to attend college, and professors, guidance counselors, and other college staff can help shape students' lives in many positive ways. But it's also possible for students to go through college without ever seriously challenging their beliefs, pushing their comfort zones, or seeing how other people live. When you combine this possibility with an incredibly high price tag, college becomes a big gamble.

If you're awarded some massive scholarship, then perhaps

you can afford this gamble. If you or your parents can foot the tuition and living bills without sacrificing sanity and security, then maybe it's okay to experiment with college.

But for everyone else—for those students and families who must make large sacrifices or take out very large loans to pay for college—the cost of this gamble is high. You don't need to pay upward of $20,000 per year to find out who you are and what you do best.

When you gamble on college, you also gamble with a second resource, one that is more precious than money: your time. Even if you can afford college, it may not be right for you. If you go to college and take little away from the experience, you will lose some of the most precious and opportunity-laden years of your life, wasting time that you could have spent traveling, starting businesses, getting exposed to new fields, pushing yourself beyond your comfort zone, and meeting new people. College is not the only place these things can happen, so if you're going there to answer the all-important question—*Who am I?*—your time may be better spent elsewhere.

Gap Years and Testing Grounds

Skipping college isn't an all-or-nothing proposition. You can treat Zero Tuition College as a gap year and simply take a one- or two-year break between high school and college.

The logic of gap years is simple. Who do you think will make a better doctor?

- Cameron, an 18-year-old who goes straight into a pre-med major from high school

- Jessica, an 18-year-old who postpones college for two years to travel across rural China (seeing real, preventable suffering), work as a ski patroller (treating actual injuries), and read books about the medical industry

But ZTC doesn't only give you experience. You can also think of it as a testing ground. For example, what if Jessica realizes that medicine is not her raison d'être and ends up in Shanghai doing graphic design? Or writing dispatches about the mining industry? Or working at a medical device startup?

Then her gap years have paid off. By taking time to test her assumptions, she has saved herself (and her family) a tremendous amount of money, time, and trouble.

Some people think that the opportunity to become a doctor justifies a heavy gamble. "You'll have time later to explore yourself," they say. To them, delaying college is irresponsible; instead, you should move forward as fast as possible.

But if your goal is long-term happiness and security, then self-knowledge is the best investment you can make. There's virtually no penalty for starting college a few years later than normal. Yet if you start college "when you're supposed to" but have no idea why you're there, this blunder comes with a huge penalty—wasted time and potentially massive debt.

Make no mistake: society needs college-trained doctors, PhDs, architects, engineers, and (not quite so many) lawyers. And some 18-year-olds have the experience necessary to jump directly into these fields. They've seen the inside of a profession, and they feel a deep calling. But most don't.

Other students jump into a licensed profession and get lucky: they go to college for four, six, or eight years, enter the workplace, and find satisfaction. They pay back their loans while enjoying their work.

But what about the rest? Maybe their gamble locks them into a profession that doesn't align with their talents or deepest interests and values. Maybe they discover a workplace that's riddled by bureaucracy, is not conducive to happiness, or is quickly becoming outsourced. But they lack the freedom to explore the world, research new job markets, start businesses, take unpaid internships, or undertake long-term retraining because they're saddled with student debt. So they choose instead to labor in unhappiness. The net result of all this gambling, of course, is a world filled with dissatisfied workers.

The solution? Don't borrow tens (or hundreds) of thousands of dollars to certify yourself in a profession about which you know nothing. Build your self-knowledge. Explore the world, earn some money, read your heart out, try many different types of work, and carefully research your college options. Call it a "gap year," "Zero Tuition College," "market research," "time off," or whatever else works for you. There's no need to rush.

Financial Security Without College, Part One

Without traditional college credentials, how can you secure a place in the modern economy? Let's begin to answer this question by discussing what the modern economy looks like—and where it's going.

You've probably heard that we are living in a "high-tech era" that requires college-level skills. That's the rationale for everyone (including you) to get a college degree—and maybe a graduate degree too. But, as economist Alan Blinder explains, this may be a dangerous oversimplification:

> Many people blithely assume that the critical distinction [in the workplace] is, and will remain, between highly educated (or highly skilled) people and less-educated (or less-skilled) people—doctors versus call-center operators, for example. The supposed remedy for the rich countries, accordingly, is more education and a general "upskilling" of the work force. But this view may be mistaken. . . . The critical divide in the future may instead be between those types of work that are easily deliverable through a wire (or via wireless connections) . . . and those that are not.[11]

Blinder is saying that modern technology changes everything. For example, when a hospital used to take an X-ray, it relied upon an in-house doctor to examine the X-ray. Today, that same hospital can send the X-ray to radiologists in India

---

11 Alan S. Blinder, "Offshoring: The Next Industrial Revolution?" *Foreign Affairs*, March/April 2006, http://www.foreignaffairs.com/articles/61514/alan-s-blinder/offshoring-the-next-industrial-revolution.

who will examine the scan for a fraction of the cost of a US doctor (especially in the middle of the night, when US doctors are sleeping but their Indian colleagues are not). Radiology is a field that requires both high skills and high education, yet it's not a highly secure form of work—because X-rays can be easily transmitted through a wire.

Now consider automotive repair, a so-called low-skill field that doesn't require a college degree. Because a real-life human is still important for diagnosing and fixing car problems, no one in a foreign country can compete with a mechanic in the United States—and therefore the job is more secure. Communication technology doesn't radically destabilize the automotive repair market, despite its "low-skill" and "low-education" status.[12]

Another way to look at the stability of different types of careers, according to the economist Frank Levy, is to consider instead whether they are rules-based or not.[13]

Work that is rules-based can be broken down into a set of established instructions that lead to a clearly defined final product. Assembling electronics, printing books, and flipping hamburgers are all examples of rules-based work.

Work that's not rules-based has no required path, set instructions, or clearly defined final product. Non-rules-

---

12 According to Blinder, you may also think of this as the distinction between "personal services"—e.g., automotive repair—and "impersonal services" like radiology. One demands a physical presence; the other doesn't. Many of the arguments in this chapter were inspired by Matthew Crawford's excellent analysis in his book, *Shop Class as Soulcraft: An Inquiry Into the Value of Work* (New York: Penguin, 2009), 33–34.

13 Frank Levy, "Education and Inequality in the Creative Age," *Cato Unbound*, June 9, 2006, http://www.cato-unbound.org/2006/06/09/frank-levy/educa-tion-and-inequality-in-the-creative-age.

based work—such as design, art, writing, marketing, and many technology jobs—demands creative thinking.

Clearly, non-rules-based work is a safer bet for people in developed nations. Daniel Pink explains:

> During the twentieth century, most work was algorithmic [rules-based]—and not just jobs where you turned the same screw the same way all day long. Even when we traded blue collars for white, the tasks we carried out were often routine. That is, we could reduce much of what we did—in accounting, law, computer programming, and other fields—to a script, a spec sheet, a formula, or a series of steps that produced a right answer. But today, in much of North America, Western Europe, Japan, South Korea, and Australia, routine white-collar work is disappearing. It's racing offshore to wherever it can be done the cheapest. In India, Bulgaria, the Philippines, and other countries, lower-paid workers essentially run the algorithm, figure out the correct answer, and deliver it instantaneously from their computer to someone six thousand miles away.[14]

What Pink describes above is offshoring, a term with which you are probably familiar. Using modern communication technology, foreign workers can easily take over the rules-based work available in developed nations. Between these communication advances and the development of automation—the replacement of human labor with machines—modern technology is rapidly transforming the modern economic landscape. According to Pink:

---

14 Daniel H. Pink, *Drive: The Surprising Truth About What Motivates Us* (New York: Riverhead, 2009), 28.

> Just as oxen and then forklifts replaced simple physical labor, computers are replacing simple intellectual labor . . . software can already perform many rule-based, professional functions better, more quickly, and more cheaply than we can. That means your cousin the CPA, if he's doing mostly routine work, faces competition not just from five-hundred-dollars-a-month accountants in Manila, but from tax preparation programs that anyone can download for thirty dollars.[15]

What do these trends mean for you, the young person who wants to explore the world without forsaking workplace security?

It first means that finding a stable job is more complicated than simply going to college. "Secure" white-collar jobs are being offshored as quickly as "secure" blue-collar jobs are being automated. No one—not even a college graduate—is fully protected from these changes.

Second, the ability to evaluate a prospective career for its susceptibility to outsourcing and automation will prove incredibly valuable—much more so than any college degree. For many people, the most secure work will be non-rules-based (i.e., creative) and require one's physical presence (i.e., not easily delivered over a wire).

But most importantly, modern economic trends highlight a new fundamental truth: whether you like it or not, today you're an entrepreneur by default.

By "entrepreneur," I don't necessarily mean a businessperson. The term was first coined by the 18th-century French economist Richard Cantillon, who considered an entrepreneur to be any person who took risks, bore uncertainty, and

---

15 Ibid.

could not expect predictable returns on his investments.[16]

Until recently, many people have believed that only self-described entrepreneurs (e.g., business owners and freelancers) are risk-takers while salaried employees are shielded from uncertainty. But anyone who witnessed the 2008 recession saw huge numbers of supposedly safe government and corporate positions slashed, manufacturing jobs disappear, grants evaporate, and retirement accounts halve. It may be clichéd to declare that we live in an "age of uncertainty," but it's clichéd because it's true. Risk-free employment simply doesn't exist. And in such an age, only entrepreneurs can cope effectively, regardless of whether they work for themselves or for someone else.

Can you gain entrepreneurial skills and attitudes in college? Perhaps—but it's unlikely. Another way to think of an entrepreneur is as someone who creates products or services of real value and who markets them to real people, all while facing the real possibility of failure. When a college student writes a sociology paper, the audience consists of two people: the student and the person grading the paper. The paper doesn't create value for anyone outside the campus bubble. If the college student gets an F in sociology, she can sign up for the class again. While dropping out due to poor grades is possible, a large number of safety nets ensures that it is extremely unlikely. Dinner is still on the table.

Some colleges do a good job of teaching entrepreneurship because they're surrounded by communities of actual

---

16 Nadim Ahmad and Richard G. Seymour, "Defining Entrepreneurial Activity: Definitions Supporting Frameworks for Data Collection," *OECD Statistics Working Papers* (2008): 1–2, 7–8, http://www.oecd.org/dataoecd/2/62/39651330.pdf.

entrepreneurs who are willing to collaborate with colleges to offer quality classes, lectures and programs (both Silicon Valley in California and Boston, Massachusetts, offer such communities). Some colleges provide the time and space for extracurricular activities that do generate real value for real people. But, overwhelmingly, the ivory tower of academia floats over the day-to-day concerns of value-producing entrepreneurs. And thanks to tenure, professors seek out and profit from a state of nearly risk-free employment. The result: most colleges don't teach entrepreneurship.

A higher education that actually helps you build economic resilience will teach you to embrace uncertainty, learn from your failures, quickly identify new opportunities, and know yourself well. It will prepare you to blaze your own path when the market crashes, the pink slip arrives, or the industry moves overseas. You can't rely on college to give you such an education; you must give one to yourself.

Financial Security Without College, Part Two

How do self-directed learners actually make their livings? Can they earn a decent amount of money? Who has taken this path successfully?

In the next section, there are a number of stories about self-directed learners who skipped or dropped out of college, but for now let's focus on one story that succinctly illustrates the answers to these questions.

Ben Hayes, a lifelong unschooler from New York City, spent much of his youth playing games of all types—video games, computer games, board games, and card games. At age 13, he got an internship at Gamelab, a NYC-based game design company. After Ben spent three years building his skills and demonstrating his value, Gamelab hired the 16-year-old as a full-fledged designer and started paying him a steady income.

At the same time, Ben was intensively playing Magic: The Gathering (a card game), working his way up through the tournament system. He soon became one of the top-ranked Magic players, a position that allowed him to explore the world as he traveled to international competitions.

When he turned 17, it seemed logical to Ben to give college a shot. He applied to Parsons, a design school, and was awarded a merit-based scholarship, but after one semester, the choice seemed wrong. Ben transferred to another NYC-based college for a semester, but his classes continued to leave him unsatisfied. He decided to go back to focusing on what he loved: building and playing games. Ben is now 21 and works as the lead designer for Playmatics, a computer gaming startup.

While self-directed learners must embrace their inner

entrepreneurs in order to find financial security, they don't necessarily have to start businesses to make a living. Many, like Ben, simply take jobs that match their passions. (You'll find concrete guidance for landing a job without a degree in the chapter entitled "Market Yourself.") After building a solid track record with one or two companies, self-directed learners possess real work experience—an asset that employers value greatly—and their nontraditional educations become a nonconcern. In fact, their backgrounds can often become a valuable, distinguishing factor during the hiring process.

Another way that self-directed learners make a living is by focusing on what they love, building mastery, and then producing a respected piece of work. They publish articles, build websites, film short movies, code software, or create art, and, when their work garners the attention of a wider community, they figure out how to use their newfound audience to make a living of some kind. Sometimes they perform or compete in a major venue; sometimes their accomplishments go viral on the Internet.

Many self-directed learners do start their own businesses. Sometimes these businesses are wildly successful (think Mark Zuckerberg and Bill Gates), but more often they're small and simple yet generate enough money to let a young adult live independently, travel often, and do what he loves. By embracing entrepreneurship at an early age, self-directed learners give themselves enough time for trial and error so that they can build a reliably profitable enterprise.

Sometimes self-directed learning instead leads you back in the direction of formal education, and you find yourself in a cooking school, long-term apprenticeship, high-level training program, or, yes, even a focused college program that provides a route to profitable employment.

Finally, many people who don't go to college gain competency in a hands-on vocation that's universally valued and unlikely to ever be offshored or automated, such as health services, construction, electrical work, landscaping, cooking, or small-scale farming. They then use the vocation as a part-time income generator or temporary back-up job.

For example, after I finished my self-directed college program (which handed me a degree but absolutely no job opportunities), I took two short and inexpensive courses that trained me as an Emergency Medical Technician and Wilderness First Responder, positions that I then used to work as a medic for summer camps and outdoor education programs. I also exploited my ability to cook for large groups—a skill I taught myself while in college—to earn money in food service while I was working on my writing.

Most college-skipping self-directed learners pursue many of these paths at once. Just as Ben Hayes focused on paid employment while also competing in Magic tournaments and experimenting with college, you can work toward creating a respected piece of work, build a small business, seek meaningful employment, and develop a vocation all at the same time. By keeping multiple opportunities open, self-directed learners build their financial security without forsaking their interests and values in the process.

* * *

What about money? Don't college graduates make more money than nongraduates? On average, yes, they do. But there are a few important caveats.

In a 2007 report, the nonprofit college-preparation organization College Board stated that college graduates make

$800,000 more in their lifetimes than their non-college-educated counterparts. However, they retracted the number in 2009; the author of the report said that $450,000 may be a more reasonable estimate.[17] When including the costs of student loan payments, forsaken work opportunities, and ballooning tuition fees, the number may even be as low as $280,000.[18] This is still a significant figure, but it is not nearly as much as we've been popularly led to believe.

The "average" lifetime earning gap also conceals a huge income variation based on one's college and field of study. Petroleum engineering majors can easily earn twice the income of child and family studies majors. Princeton and MIT graduates typically earn three times as much as Coker College alumni.[19] Graduates with liberal arts degrees from noncompetitive colleges may well earn less than sales managers, real estate brokers, and other people whose positions don't require a college degree.[20]

Here are a few more reasons why the lifetime earning gap between graduates and nongraduates shouldn't scare you:

---

17 Mary Pilon, "What's a Degree Really Worth?" *Wall Street Journal*, February 2, 2010, http://online.wsj.com/article/SB10001424052748703822404575019 082819966538.html.

18 Ibid.

19 "Degrees That Pay You Back" and "Salary Potential By School Location," 2011–2012 PayScale College Salary Report, PayScale, accessed February 20, 2012, http://www.payscale.com/best-colleges.

20 "20 Great Jobs That Don't Require a Degree," CNN (CareerBuilder), posted February 24, 2006, http://www.cnn.com/2006/US/Careers/02/24/cb.no. degree.jobs.

   Specific income figures from various colleges, majors, and professions change annually, so I've tried to make statements that will generally hold constant. Crunch your own numbers by visiting sites like PayScale.com or searching online for average earnings.

- When you don't include graduates of the Ivy Leagues and other elite colleges, the gap in average lifetime income narrows even more.

- Income is not the same thing as wealth. Many college graduates (and adults in general) may have high incomes, but they might also be up to their ears in debt.

- Earning a high income can become a detriment to learning how to live frugally, which is an incredibly valuable life skill in the age of the entrepreneur.

- Money is just money; time is life's true commodity. If you're going to college in pursuit of some mythical six-figure income, that's a poor gamble to make with four precious years. On the other hand, pursuing an adventurous, self-directed education guarantees you a value-filled experience.

*   *   *

Finally, it helps to hear the names of a few people who didn't complete college but are still widely considered to be successful. Here's a list of such people—one for each letter of the alphabet, except X and Y—adapted from John Kremer's excellent website, "The College Dropouts Hall of Fame."[21]

---

21 John Kremer, "The College Dropouts Hall of Fame," accessed December 20, 2011, http://www.collegedropoutshalloffame.com. Adapted with permission of creator.

   For more stories of wildly successful nongraduates, see Michael Ellsberg's *The Education of Millionaires* (New York: Portfolio, 2011).

Allen, Paul. Cofounder of Microsoft. Dropped out of the University of Washington to work for Honeywell. A year later he convinced Bill Gates to drop out of Harvard and move to Albuquerque, New Mexico, to start Microsoft.

Bacon, Kevin. Actor, singer, and songwriter. At the age of 17, he dropped out of high school and moved to New York City to pursue a career as an actor.

Carson, Julia. US Congress representative, and Indiana's second African-American woman elected to Congress. Did not graduate from college.

DeGeneres, Ellen. Comedian, actress, and talk show host. Dropped out of the University of New Orleans.

Ecko, Mark. Founder of Mark Ecko Enterprises, an urbanwear company. Left Rutgers University during his third year to start the company with his sister, Marci, who also left college to work on the business.

Fields, Debbi. Founded Mrs. Fields Cookies when she was a 21-year-old mother with no business experience. Did not graduate from college.

Graf, Steffi. Tennis star. Turned professional in her teens when she ran out of players good enough to challenge her. Never attended college.

Hoffer, Eric. Author (*The True Believer*). A self-educated philosopher, he was at various times a dishwasher, lumberjack, gold prospector, migrant farm worker, and longshoreman.

Imus, Don. National radio host and bestselling author. Dropped out of college after a week.

Jones, Jeremy. Snowboarder and film star. Did not attend college. Moved to Jackson Hole, Wyoming, to pursue his passion as a snowboarder.

Kubrick, Stanley. Movie director, producer, screenwriter, and photographer. His poor high school grades made it impossible for him to attend college.

Lanier, Cathy. Chief of police of Washington, DC, and the first woman to hold this position. A junior-high-school dropout and unwed mother at 15.

Mackey, John. Founder of Whole Foods. Dropped out of the University of Texas six times. Never took a business course.

Neuhaus, Richard John. Theologian, Lutheran minister, Catholic priest, author, and civil rights activist. Never graduated from high school.

Ono, Yoko. Artist and singer. Dropped out of Sarah Lawrence College.

Puck, Wolfgang. Chef and restaurateur. Quit school at the age of 14 and got a job as a cooking apprentice at a hotel.

Qualls, Ashley. Founder of Whateverlife.com, which helps people build their Myspace pages. Left high school at 15 to devote herself to her website business, through which she made more than a million dollars by the age of 17.

Rowling, J.K. Novelist (*Harry Potter* series) and first billionaire author. Never attended college.

Salinger, J.D. Novelist (*Catcher in the Rye*). Briefly attended Ursinus College and New York University before publishing short stories in *Collier's* and *Esquire*.

Truman, Harry. US president. After high school he worked at a bank, joined the National Guard, managed his family farm, served in World War I, and opened a haberdashery (which failed) before entering politics.[22]

Ueltschi, Albert. Billionaire founder of FlightSafety International pilot training schools. Dropped out of the University of Kentucky to fly planes and, after flying for PanAm for ten years, founded FlightSafety.

Von Drachenberg, Katherine (a.k.a. Kat Von D). Reality TV star, tattoo artist, skateboard designer, and developer of makeup line. Dropped out of school at the age of 14.

Willis, Bruce. Actor. Dropped out of the theater program of Montclair State University after his junior year.

Z, Jay (a.k.a. Shawn Carter). Rapper, entrepreneur, and owner of Rocawear clothing. Never attended college.

---

22 "Harry S. Truman," Biography.com, accessed February 25, 2012, http://www.biography.com/people/harry-s-truman-9511121.

You Can Work Hard Without College

Without college, you have incredible freedom. You choose your own projects, set your own hours, and learn at your own pace. But with this freedom also comes the need to self-motivate. College offers a comprehensive system of grades, exams, homework, and face-to-face accountability that compels students to work hard. Without such a built-in system, how will you continually motivate yourself to undertake your self-directed studies? The subfield of psychology known as positive psychology holds the solution.

Since it was started in the 1950s by psychologists Carl Rogers and Abraham Maslow, positive psychology research has focused on the factors of human life that make people more happy, talented, and productive. In recent decades, the field's most accomplished practitioners—Edward Deci, K. Anders Ericsson, Mihaly Csikszentmihalyi, and Carol Dweck—have written books that are valuable for anyone serious about becoming a self-directed learner.

Do you think you need to attend college to be motivated? According to Deci, all you actually need is an environment that promotes autonomy, mastery in a specific field, and relatedness (a sense of community). Admittedly, most colleges do offer some level of autonomy, mastery, and relatedness. But college can also become restrictive if, for example, you find a class that exposes you to a fascinating new topic, but the syllabus moves on before you can delve deeply into that issue. At that point, self-directed learning undoubtedly offers a better environment for self-motivation.[23]

---

23 Learn more about Deci's research by reading his book *Why We Do What We Do: Understanding Self-Motivation* (New York: Penguin, 1996).

Do you think you need to attend college to build deep skills? According to Ericsson, you only need deliberate practice: custom-tailored instruction accompanied by immediate, high-quality feedback. Self-directed learners recruit tutors, mentors, and coaches to provide them with deliberate practice experiences. That's how they learn to read, write, research, and gain the other skills typically associated with college.[24]

Do you think you need to attend college to learn how to work hard? According to Csikszentmihalyi, what you really need is to experience flow, a state characterized by high challenge and high achievement that makes difficult work feel effortless. And, according to Dweck, you need to learn to ask for the right kind of feedback. By reading each of their books (*Flow* and *Mindset*, respectively), you'll see how self-directed learners embrace big challenges over and over again.[25]

Even if you don't read a single page of psychology research, you can create the environment necessary for you to work hard. The next section of this book shows you the concrete steps to begin creating this environment. Follow these steps, and you'll see that the power to motivate yourself, work hard, and design the education of a lifetime is fully within your grasp.

---

24 Learn more about Ericsson's research by reading Geoff Colvin's *Talent Is Overrated* (New York: Penguin, 2008).

25 Learn more by reading Milhaly Csikszentmihalyi's *Flow: The Psychology of Optimal Experience* (New York: Harper and Row, 1990) and Carol Dweck's *Mindset: The New Psychology of Success* (New York: Random House, 2007).
    For the curious reader, Daniel Pink's *Drive* provides an excellent introduction to all of these positive psychologists. You can also find a series of related blog posts available at http://www.ztcollege.com.

WHAT TO DO INSTEAD OF COLLEGE

Five Stories

If you don't go to college, what will you do with your time? To illustrate the answers to this question, let's begin with the stories of five young adults who chose self-directed learning over college.[26]

Tara Dean

Fed up with Massachusetts public high school, Tara Dean dropped out at age 16 and began volunteering on organic farms across the United States. To prove that she wasn't a typical dropout, she took online classes through her local community college but quickly found them to be a waste of time. Instead of continuing her classes, Tara intensified her travels. She drove across the country, biked across South Africa, and backpacked across Europe. To fund her constant travel, Tara would connect each of her trips to some charitable cause and then raise money from a wide circle of friends and family. She also made good use of her family's frequent-flyer miles and earned some money working on farms.

While working on a farm in western Massachusetts, Tara learned the basics of midwifery and felt a deep pull toward it.

---

26 These stories feature young people who took alternative paths through both college and high school. I emphasize these highly nontraditional learners for two reasons. First, their stories highlight how little formal credentials (even high school diplomas) may matter in finding success. Second, very few people have documented the lives of homeschoolers and unschoolers who succeed without college, in contrast to the relatively high number of such stories about traditional high school graduates (see "Financial Security Without College, Part Two").

She contemplated starting her own birth consulting business but realized that she needed more experience before anyone would hire her. To gain expertise, Tara began integrating a number of training programs into her travels, including a midwifery conference in Pennsylvania, a neonatal resuscitation course in Tennessee, and two unpaid internships at a birth center for undocumented immigrants in Texas.

Life on the road, however, took its toll. Feeling burned out, Tara returned home at age 18 to live with her parents and continue to develop her business ideas. During that time, she built a simple website that listed her services and background. Tara decided that she needed one more big piece of experience before running her own show, so she joined a volunteer trip to Senegal where she enjoyed the opportunity to deliver dozens of babies on her own.

Now 19, Tara felt prepared to give her freelance business a shot. She moved to Asheville, North Carolina—a progressive community that seemed ripe with midwifery possibilities—and immediately started generating clients, assisting in home births, and earning money.

By taking local midwives out to tea, organizing her own natural birth education group, and living with other young adults in a community house, Tara soon found herself part of a vibrant network of peers, mentors, and clients. She updated her website to include her new services, business philosophy, testimonials, midwife-related travel photos, and community projects, making it reflect Tara's competent, high-energy, and self-directed personality.[27]

When I interviewed Tara in Asheville in late 2011, she was hopping on a plane to Costa Rica to get trained in mas-

---

27 Visit Tara's website at http://www.solunabirthservices.com.

sage therapy—another service that her business would soon offer. Transformed and enlivened by her decision to leave traditional education early on, Tara had no regrets about her decision to skip college.

Weezie Yancey-Siegel

Weezie Yancey-Siegel grew up in traditional schools, but she was part of a nontraditional, world-traveling family. As a teenager she helped create and run her family's educational nonprofit organization, lived in India for six months, and filmed her own documentaries on topics ranging from immigration to Internet culture. She started attending a small liberal arts college in 2009, but, after a year and a half, Weezie felt the need for something different. She decided to skip her junior year and instead craft her own experiential gap year.

To replace the structure to which she had become accustomed, Weezie began by writing her own syllabus. She gave herself assignments that included watching TED Talks, reading blogs, meditating, creating art, and interviewing other students. She started blogging about her activities, goals, and interviews. But after a few months of structured self-learning, Weezie put her syllabus on the back burner in order to travel across Europe. Her parents agreed to buy the plane ticket if she would earn four months' travel money, which she promptly did by babysitting, working for her grandmother's friends at a retirement home, and snagging an au pair gig in Greece.

A social media enthusiast, Weezie decided to use her online savvy to connect with locals working in her fields of interest: education and social entrepreneurship. By e-mailing the people and organizations that fascinated her, Weezie got volunteer positions at high-end conferences, met dozens of social entrepreneurs, and made herself part of the European Twitter community. Continuously blogging about her adventures, she gained a huge online following of friends, family, and European contacts who read about her travels, plans, and interviews with other "eduventurists," Weezie's term for self-directed young adults.[28]

When I interviewed Weezie near the end of her gap year, I asked her where she was finding accountability, a challenge that she openly discussed on her blog. Weezie told me that three sources kept her accountable to her stated goals: her parents, the friends following her blog (especially when they asked questions about her progress), and the "natural accountability" of undertaking meaningful challenges that she chose herself.

Throughout her gap year Weezie planned to return to college at the end. But then she had a change of heart. When I asked her why, she wrote to me:

> I realized that the type of experiential/self-designed learning I had been engaging in was a lot more beneficial to me, in that it interested and excited me, it was more relevant to the real world, and it was helping to build my résumé and contacts more so than college.

Weezie had decided not to completely rule out college because she believed that a degree might be necessary for certain fields of her interest, but she was considering transfer-

---

28 To read more about Weezie's work, visit her website, http://www.eduventurist.org.

ring to a low-residency program that better matched her new lifestyle.[29]

Sean Ritchey

Lifelong unschooler Sean Ritchey started selling, building, and managing long before he founded his own company. At age 11 he began working at a family friend's retail shop; at 14 he learned enough carpentry to help build his parents' house; and at 15 he organized benefit concerts for charities.

Late in his teens, Sean took a full load of community college classes while interning for an environmental nonprofit. He got accepted to multiple colleges but received little financial aid. He decided that the value wasn't worth the high price tag, so, instead of enrolling, he took a job with the same nonprofit, training college students to do campus energy audits.

While Sean was working with students at top schools like Vassar and Bard, administrators often tried to recruit him, but he had no interest in college life. Now 19, he decided to cofound a home building company that specialized in ultra-energy-efficient design. Deep Green Building was Sean's life for the next three years. Through this experience he both paid his bills and earned his unofficial "bachelor in entrepreneurship," building his skills in marketing, sales, project management, employee leadership, and accounting. For Sean, entrepreneurship felt like a natural evolution from being a self-directed learner.

When the economy collapsed in 2008, so did Deep Green's revenue stream. Earning money as a carpenter and building

---

29 For example, Prescott College in Arizona. Find more information about alternative and low-residency colleges at http://www.ztcollege.com.

consultant, Sean refocused his energy on working on the board of a nonprofit, creating his own nonprofit, organizing a small conference, and exploring sustainable communities across the country. To share his many experiences, Sean compiled his photos, videos, stories, project websites, blog, and social media profiles into an online portfolio.[30]

In 2011 Sean, now 24, was living with a group of friends in upstate New York. But he still wasn't settled, having just begun renovating an Airstream Land Yacht to be a high-efficiency home on wheels. His other projects included developing a leadership training program about democratic household management, working as a business startup advisor, and speaking at conferences. Living debt-free, engaged with his goals, and surrounded by a community who shared his values, Sean deeply appreciated his decision to skip college.

Brenna McBroom

A homeschooler as a child and an unschooler as a teen, Brenna McBroom read voraciously, took local theater classes, and competed in Odyssey of the Mind, team problem-solving tournaments with complex challenges like building mechanical devices and interpreting literary classics. Throughout her young adulthood, Brenna assumed that she would go to college—a goal that her parents thoroughly encouraged. In pursuit of this path, she took two years of community college classes, prepped for the SAT, and did hundreds of hours of community service. At 18, she was accepted to her top choice: New College of Florida.

---

30 To read more about Sean's work, visit his website, http://www.seanritchey. com.

But after a semester of abstract courses and watching highly credentialed New College graduates take jobs at Whole Foods, Brenna began to suspect that school wasn't giving her marketable life skills. The title of one of her first course papers, "Hume's Positive View Concerning the Non-Rationality of Causal Inferences," troubled her. "After college, no one cares how well you can talk about Hume and Kant," Brenna remembers thinking.

Adding to her frustration was an unfulfilled desire to create ceramic art. A few weeks before starting college, Brenna had taken a course in wheel-thrown ceramics and fallen deeply in love with it. Whenever she returned home from college for a weekend, she would throw a dozen pots, mugs, and teapots. Halfway through her first year, New College let Brenna design a ceramics-oriented independent study. But when she tried to create another ceramics course the following semester, no professors would sponsor her. At that point Brenna realized that her college could not give her what she wanted most: experience in high-level ceramics. She researched bachelor of fine arts (BFA) programs but found that they required far more general education courses than actual ceramics instruction.

Brenna gave New College one more shot, returning for the first week of classes of sophomore year. That weekend, sitting face to face with a stack of articles about queer theory that seemed impossibly dense, incomprehensible, and irrelevant, Brenna decided to leave so that she could follow her passion for ceramic art.[31]

Even though she had a full scholarship, Brenna left New

---

31 Brenna was the unschooler who left her liberal arts school as described in "My Story."

College that weekend, and her parents supported her decision. But the fact that she had worked so hard to get into college left Brenna with a minor identity crisis. She spent the next five months living at her parents' house in a depressed funk. She threw pots and struggled to remember what self-directed learning felt like.

The tides changed when she traveled to Cambridge, Massachusetts, for a month-long apprenticeship under a master potter. Now able to throw bigger pieces in less time, Brenna created a small revenue stream by selling her work on the website Etsy.com. She used this money to build a business website, travel to India, and sell more pottery at nationwide conferences and local art festivals.[32] More significantly, she began to take herself seriously as a ceramic artist and regained faith in her self-directed path.

In 2011, at age 22, Brenna had just completed another high-intensity apprenticeship, this time in the ceramics technique called "crystalline glazing," and she had begun selling pieces for more than $100. While she took the occasional part-time job to help pay the bills, she lived on her own and worked on ceramics for 40 hours each week.

Allen Ellis

Allen Ellis grew up in rural Pennsylvania in a home-schooling-turned-unschooling family who surrounded him with opportunities. He took piano and horseback riding lessons, competed in chess tournaments, attended Space Camp in Florida, and managed a small snack bar. These opportuni-

---

32 Visit Brenna's website at http://www.brennadee.com.

ties came with hardships, too: when Allen was 11, his father passed away from cancer.

As a teenager, Allen spent hours playing with digital video cameras, building web pages, gaming, programming, and filming short movies. When he was 14, his mom nudged him into asking for an internship with a local video production company; a half-dozen "really nice e-mails" later, Allen secured the position. (He later realized that the internship was meant for college students, but the company hired him because he seemed "the most dedicated.") He took a handful of business-oriented community college classes, and, at 17, he secured an internship at his local megachurch, where he was required to produce videos under strict deadlines. When his mentor was suddenly fired, Allen became the church's one-man multimedia department. "Being thrust into a situation where so many people needed and trusted me felt incredible," Allen told me. "I'm confident that no curriculum could have possibly replaced that."

Now nearing 19, he found a college multimedia program that promised "real-life" training on industry-grade equipment. Allen had always assumed that he would end up in such a program—and he was excited by the opportunity to work with supportive teams on a large scale—yet he hesitated to enroll. "I was engaged enough in my own projects that the prospect of putting everything on hold for four years felt counterintuitive." More importantly to Allen, the other students in the program just didn't seem thrilled to be there. So instead of enrolling, he seized opportunities to travel across Argentina and Thailand.

Upon returning stateside, Allen convinced a childhood friend to move with him to Tennessee and renovate his family's rental house. Together they drew up a budget, hired contractors, and put in the hands-on work necessary to repair and sell the house in three months. Soon after, his grandmother's disabilities forced her to move to a nursing home, and Allen moved into her vacant house in Orlando, Florida, to support her. With no rent payments and no student debt, Allen used his freedom to volunteer with Habitat for Humanity, start a spirituality discussion group, and found a freelance multimedia design service.[33] Soon his freelance life took off. Through a Habitat for Humanity conference, Allen met a professional magician, filmed him, got invited to the magician's networking event, and started doing graphic and web work for new clients across the country.

Before too long, Allen discovered a local company that designed multimedia for national conferences and awards ceremonies. Thrilled by the scope of their work, he e-mailed the company every month for almost a year, pointing them toward his online portfolio and expressing his eagerness to be a part of their operation. "The day I got the invitation to join them for my first project was incredible," Allen said. Now 22, he works at the company full-time, in a senior position on a small but growing team. His parting thought:

> As we hire new employees and interns, it's staggering to me how few know or care what job they want to do. Even in this economy, it's hard to find people who are both passionate and skilled. I can only see truth in the statement, "Do what you love, and the money will follow."

---

33 Visit Allen's portfolio at http://www.allenellis.com.

The ZTC Strategy

What did Tara, Weezie, Sean, Brenna, and Allen do to find their ways without college? How can you do the same?

Successful college-skippers follow a pattern. If you follow it too, you can find success without college. I call this pattern the ZTC strategy.

Here's the blueprint:

First, BUILD SELF-KNOWLEDGE. Figure out what deeply interests and drives you.

Second, GIVE YOURSELF ASSIGNMENTS. Undertake big projects, read books, do internships, start businesses, practice extensively, and find other ways to increase your knowledge and skills.

Third, CREATE AND SHARE VALUE. Volunteer, get hired, or sell your work. Organize groups, plan events, or start small movements. Write, blog, film, code, or photograph. Dedicate your time to building things that other people find valuable, and then share them with the world.

Fourth, FIND SUPPORT. To intelligently navigate your self-directed life, seek the guidance, mentorship, and friendship of adults and peers. Ask them to keep you accountable to what you say you'll do.

Finally, MARKET YOURSELF. Build an online portfolio that tells your story, displays your accomplishments, and makes you easy to find. Expand your network by being genuinely helpful to those in need, and learn how to land jobs through referrals and other creative means.

*   *   *

We'll walk through the ZTC strategy in the order presented above, but you shouldn't necessarily follow it in that order. Many steps of the strategy enable and reinforce the others: assignments generate self-knowledge, finding support helps you create value, and value creation helps you market yourself. To begin your self-directed journey, focus on the part of the ZTC strategy that you need most.

Build Self-Knowledge

Where do you want to go in this world? What's important? How will you contribute? Tara, Weezie, Sean, Brenna, and Allen could not have taken the first step along their journeys without this information.

There's no magical formula for building self-knowledge. Getting exposed to new people, places, and ideas when you're young helps, as does spending time in solitary, unguided contemplation (e.g., traveling, walking, camping, and meditation). But virtually every experience is an opportunity to build self-knowledge. At any moment, as the psychologist Abraham Maslow said, "You will either step forward into growth or you will step back into safety."[34] What separates self-directed learners from other people is their clear intention to step forward into growth as often as possible.

Regardless of the origin of self-knowledge, you unquestionably possess some of it, and that is what you must draw upon to begin your self-directed path. Start by asking yourself these three questions:

1. If you were going to die one year from today, what would you do differently?

2. If you had three years to create something that would change your world, how would you begin?

---

34 Brian Johnson, "Inspirational Quotes: Abraham Maslow," *Brian Johnson's PhilosophersNotes*, accessed March 7, 2012, http://www.philosophersnotes.com/quotes/by_teacher/Abraham%20Maslow.

3. If you were forbidden from accumulating vast mate-
    rial wealth, how would you live differently?

To understand these questions better, let's look at each of
them in more depth.

If you were going to die one year from today, what would you do differently?

Without the "I'm in school" excuse, you can immediately
start doing what you feel is most important. If you were to
die in a year, what plans would you make today? Would you
visit an intriguing part of the world, write a book, or start a
company? Would you build (or repair) a certain relationship?
Who would you spend your time with? Which long-deferred
goals and dreams would you begin working on? What dis-
tractions would you cut from your life?

This question's shortcoming, of course, is that it forecloses
the possibility of long-term aspirations. In all likelihood you're
going to live a long, healthy life. Thus the next question:

If you had three years to create something that would change your world, how would you begin?

Define "your world" as you wish. It may mean your neigh-
borhood, a community of enthusiasts, a group whose cause
you believe in, or strangers across the globe. How could you
positively impact these people within three years while also
doing something that you love? Dream on a grander scale
than you did for the previous question. Perhaps you would
film a documentary, build a coalition of businesses and non-
profits, or organize a conference. What kind of training and

knowledge would you need to make this dream happen? Whose mentorship could you seek?

If you were forbidden from accumulating vast material wealth, how would you live differently?

Imagine that you took an irrevocable vow of frugality. You can have a car, rental house, computer, and other basic assets (by the standards of a developed country), but not a boat, fancy mountain bike, expensive jewelry, or savings beyond six months' living expenses. You're barred from ever owning such luxuries, and you can't sneak around this rule with clever tactics like offshore accounts or asking your friends to hold your money. Of course, you can keep all of the intangible stuff in your life: your projects, reputation, relationships, knowledge, and memories. But you'll never be materially rich.

Living under this ironclad law of frugality, what would you focus your energy on? How would your vision of success change?

* * *

Really think about these three big questions and then write down your answers on your computer, a piece of paper, a napkin, or your arm. Don't keep the answers locked in your head; it will be too easy to not take them seriously.

Now ask yourself: How far-fetched are these scenarios? And why shouldn't I begin acting upon my answers?

It's possible that you will discover tomorrow that you have cancer and have a year left to live. You could die in a car accident a year from today. Living only for the future is no way to live; you must pay attention to your most pressing short-term dreams. Your answers to the first question deserve a place in your life.

Yet the future matters, too, because you're probably going to live a long life. And to live in a market economy, everyone must create something of value, whether it is a product, service, or Subway sandwich. What you create will somehow change the world (even if it's just a sandwich). So within three years, you will have changed the world—but how? In a way that promotes your vision of positive change? Someone else's vision? Or no vision at all? If you don't start building the world in which you want to live, then that world may never exist. Your answers to the second question deserve serious attention.

Finally, in a world of ever-present economic uncertainty, preparing yourself to live a frugal life isn't a terrible idea. The modern economy offers incredible opportunities for creating vast amounts of wealth, and understanding how to harness such opportunities is important. But you may find it difficult to protect your accumulated wealth. That's why providing for your basic needs in creative ways is a reality worth preparing for. Choosing the ZTC path certainly doesn't prevent you from becoming wealthy, as we saw in "Financial Security Without College, Part Two." But instead of focusing on maximizing your assets, you'll benefit more by focusing on maximizing your experiences.

Look again at your answers to the above questions. This is the foundation of self-knowledge on which your life rests, and it's where your life without college begins.

Give Yourself Assignments

Armed with self-knowledge, you can now design your ZTC assignments, the specific self-directed projects that will build your higher education.

What elements go into a strong self-directed project? What differentiates a ZTC assignment from casual exploration or a traditional college assignment? Every assignment that you give yourself should be:

- centered around your interests and goals (whether long-term or short-term),

- exciting enough to motivate you,

- challenging enough to demand growth,

- focused (with a clear goal), and

- self-contained (with a clear beginning and end).[35]

Consider the implications of this list. If you give yourself an assignment:

- because it's expected of you (by friends, parents, or society), then it's not truly a self-directed assignment.

- that's too easy, then it won't excite or challenge you. Real ZTC assignments feel ambitious, enlivening, and a little scary.

---

35 To learn how to write highly specific assignments for yourself, use the technique that I call "Dream Mapping," available at http://www.ztcollege.com.

- that's unfocused, you won't really know where to begin or when you're done. The assignment "Become a smarter person," for example, would be almost impossible to start—and definitely impossible to finish.

Crafting strong self-directed assignments is an art. As with all art, it helps to mimic others at first. Outlined below are the types of assignments toward which many self-directed learners gravitate—and you may too. Because the following assignments are written for a broad audience, they don't model the focus and specificity of an excellent assignment, but you'll find a few examples of more specific assignments at the end of each description.

An asterisk indicates that you can find resources (websites, books, articles, companies, etc.) related to this assignment or activity at http://www.ztcollege.com.

Travel the World

Visiting new cultures and lands is one of the oldest and best ways to meet new people, clear your mind, prioritize your life, have fun, and learn something about the cultural lens through which you see the world. To begin:

- Consider exploring the most foreign culture that you can bear. If you're North American, then traveling to Western Europe will be easy—maybe too easy. Remember that a strong assignment must be challenging enough to demand growth.

- Research and prepare for your trip by reading guidebooks, travel blogs, and websites.*

- Start learning the language of your destination with a course or software program. For more widespread languages like Spanish, French, German, and Chinese, consider hiring a local language tutor. For almost any language, you can also use Skype to work with overseas tutors who will coach you in their native languages.*

- Browse CouchSurfing.org, HelpX.net, and WWOOF. org to find inexpensive opportunities to meet, stay with, and volunteer with local people. Old-fashioned social skills like saying "hello" help too.*

- Do one good deed for a person in need on your travels.

- Blog each day (with both writing and photos) and share it with friends, family, travel websites, and your social network.

Total costs:

- Budget travel ($500–1500 per month, depending on destination, activities, and travel costs)

- Language learning ($0 for library books and free online practice; $100–300 for classes, tutoring, and/or software)

- Volunteering, connecting with locals, and doing good deeds ($0)

- Blogging ($0)

Examples:

- "Learn 100 words of basic Hindi and connect with 10 new people while traveling across India for a month."

- "Live and work in New Zealand for three months, couchsurfing and using volunteering sites to spend less than $500 per month."

Find a Vocation

Vocational work is anything that engages both your hands and mind while fulfilling a community need. Most vocational work can't be offshored or automated, making it an excellent money-making or bartering opportunity. And in our age of "knowledge work," working outside or with your hands provides much-needed relief from a computer screen. To begin:

- Ask yourself what training or experience you already possess. Do you have a skill that fulfills a community need? Will the work soon be sent overseas or done by a machine? Does it genuinely interest you?

- Increase your skills by taking an instructional course or entry-level job or by working with a mentor or master practitioner. Community colleges might provide excellent, inexpensive training courses.

- Consider offering your service freelance or as part of a small business. Before doing that, get three strong letters of recommendation from bosses, mentors, teachers, or clients, and have a friend take photos or videos of you working. Start a simple website that describes your services and includes the media and letters of recommendation.

Total costs:

- Skills training (variable)

- Letters of recommendation ($0)[36]

- Photos, videos, and simple website ($0-50)

Examples:

- "Learn how to do basic carpentry, plumbing, and electrical home repair work by watching YouTube videos, reading books, and volunteering to tackle basic repairs for my friends."

- "Work with a local chef to build the skills necessary to prepare and sell gluten-free meals as a freelance personal chef."

Become a Public Intellectual

Public intellectuals research, think, talk, and write about a social problem but don't necessarily hold formal credentials. They spread their messages via blogs, websites, books, magazines, podcasts, videos, and other media platforms. To begin:

---

36 Letters of recommendation need not be physical pieces of paper. You can ask for recommendations via e-mail and then copy and paste them into your online portfolio. This also goes for referrals and testimonials.

- Research a social problem that you care about deeply. Get your facts straight, learn the history of the arguments, and then take a stand on the issue.[37]

- Start a blog. Ask a web-savvy friend to make it look professional, and write a few pilot posts. Solicit feedback from the smartest people you know, hone your writing, and revise your ideas. Consider hiring a professional editor if ample support isn't available in your community.* Repeat multiple times before going public.

- Alternatively, express your thoughts in audio or video format. Use a similarly rigorous feedback process.

- When you're ready to spread the word, share your work via social media and by sending friendly e-mails to leaders in your field. (More advice on this element can be found in the "Find Support" chapter.)

- Consider expanding your work into an e-book, article series, or full-fledged manuscript.*

Total costs:

- Research, web hosting, and content expansion ($0-50)

- Soliciting feedback on your work ($0 with friends and acquaintances; $100–500 with professional editors)

---

37 Remember that any public stand you take on a controversial issue will probably never disappear from the Internet. Don't publish anything that you'll regret later when a potential employer googles you.

Examples:

- "Write a blog post of 1000–2000 words, send it to three bloggers whose work I admire, and follow their suggestions until one agrees to publish it as a guest post."

- "Get in touch with two podcasters whom I admire, ask them for startup advice, and produce my own podcast (half hour or longer)."

Teach a Course

A Chinese proverb says: "Tell me and I'll forget; show me and I may remember; involve me and I'll understand." But if you've ever taught before, you know that one more phrase belongs here: "Have me teach it, and I'll really know my stuff."

Leading a course or workshop (whether in-person or online) is a fantastic way to solidify and demonstrate your understanding of a specific topic. To begin:

- Choose a subject or skill about which you are knowledgeable. You don't have to be a world-class expert; you just need to be better than your students.

- Ask yourself which medium or venue you prefer. Would you rather record a series of instructional videos, offer an online course, lead a hands-on class, tutor an individual or small group, or create a workshop for a conference?*

- Prepare and do a test-run of your course, workshop, or instructional materials with a willing volunteer.

- In the beginning, offer your course for free to build experience and references. Charge only what you need to cover the cost of space and materials. As you gain more experience, begin charging for your time as well.

- If leading a course in person, ask someone to document your instruction with photo or video.

- After finishing your first course, obtain five or more letters of recommendation from your students/ participants, if possible.

Total costs:

- Online venue ($0)* or local venue (variable; ideally covered by course fees)

- Prepping and testing your course ($0)

- Documentation and letters of support ($0)

Examples:

- "Prepare and pitch a workshop to [a specific conference I'd like to attend] so that I can go for free or for a discounted rate."

- "Lead a free three-week course on harnessing social media for my local writers' group."

Create a Small Enterprise

A successful enterprise (whether a business, one-time event, community group, or other type of organization) always begins with the question, "Why hasn't anyone done this yet?" Do you know of a community, either local or online, with unfulfilled needs? If so, you can start a small enterprise. It does not need to be profitable in the beginning, but it should feel like a productive and rewarding use of your time. To begin:

- Volunteer, intern, or work for an organization or event similar to the one you wish to create. Gain an insider's perspective.

- Clearly identify your future customers or participants: who are they, how will they find your enterprise, and why will they spend their time and money with you instead of elsewhere? If you can't clearly answer these questions, don't jump in yet.

- Interview three accomplished people who have started enterprises that you admire and ask for their advice.

- Research the legal structure (e.g., sole proprietorship, limited liability company) that your enterprise will require in order to accept payments. Some very small enterprises or one-time events won't require any legal structure.*

- Find and read books, articles, and other resources centered on the nitty-gritty of starting your specific type of enterprise.

- Start selling/providing your product or service on a very small scale. Do this before spending a single cent on formally establishing your enterprise (unless absolutely necessary to protect yourself from high liability).

- If people like what you're offering, then spend the money necessary to become legal and legitimate.

Total costs:

- Volunteering/interning/working for a similar enterprise, conducting interviews, reading and researching ($0)

- Startup costs (highly variable, but probably less than $500 for a business without physical inventory)

Examples:

- "Organize a small regional conference around a topic relevant to my community. Aim for 200–300 attendees."

- "Start a bicycle lunch delivery service that takes orders via Twitter and text message."

Explore the World of Ideas

Most four-year liberal arts colleges insist that their students explore a wide range of academic subjects. In general, this is a good idea. But why limit yourself to the subjects offered at a specific college? As a self-directed learner, you can assign yourself the task of constantly exploring new fields, both academic and nonacademic. To begin:

- Ask your social networks and the smartest people you know to recommend interesting books, websites, blogs, articles, podcasts, movies, and videos—especially those that don't match your preexisting interests and biases.

- Open yourself to something completely new and unpredictable. Click the "Featured Content" or "Random Article" links on Wikipedia. Spend an evening exploring a university library or bookstore.*

- Watch TED Talks.*

- Browse free audio and video recordings of the classes of top professors.*

- If you're near a college campus, consider sitting in on a class. Most professors are happy to let you sample a few of their classes if you ask permission first (via e-mail or phone).

Total costs:

- Accessing the wide world of ideas via library browsing, campus visits, or the Internet: $0. (Isn't that wonderful?)

Examples:

- "Find three articles that intelligently challenge my preconceived political, religious, or philosophical beliefs."

- "Undertake an Ivy League course that's offered for free online. Rigorously follow its curriculum, and write a daily blog post about my experience."

*   *   *

These are just a few of the meaningful and exciting assignments that you might give yourself as you build your self-directed higher education. To generate more possibilities, think about your answers to the previous chapter's questions ("What would you do if you were going to die in a year," etc.). With these—and the guidelines for assignments explained above—you can begin crafting your own ZTC assignments.

When considering cost, don't forget to take into account the time necessary for the assignment. Time, not money, is the ultimate nonrenewable resource. Never undertake an assignment simply because it's cheap; do it because it's the best possible use of your time.[38]

Now compile your assignments in the form of a syllabus, goal list, or other format. I'll soon make the case for posting your assignments online for friends, family, and the general public to see, so consider keeping your list on the computer. I'll also explain how to keep yourself accountable to your biggest (and most intimidating) assignments.

Don't worry about planning four whole years; it's good enough to plan three, six, or nine months into the future. One of the big advantages of self-directed learning is that when a golden opportunity arises—to travel abroad, join a fast-moving business team, or get involved in a meaningful project—you have the freedom to seize it quickly.

---

38 I'm indebted to unschooling advocate Diane Flynn Keith for emphasizing the importance of this piece of advice.

Create and Share Value

Self-directed learning comes in many different flavors, from reading a book to traveling the world. But a ZTC assignment is a specific kind of challenge that generates work opportunities and self-knowledge very quickly. What makes ZTC assignments special? For the answer, consider the story of Vi Hart.

Vi studied music at Stony Brook University but practiced math on the side—a hobby inspired by her father, a computer science professor who began taking her to math conferences when she was 13. After graduating from Stony Brook, Vi spent two years trying to figure out how to combine her music training with her lifelong love of math. Facing slim job prospects as a self-described "recreational mathemusician," Vi created a simple video about doodling in math class that "married a distaste for the way math is taught in school with an exuberant exploration of math as art"—in the words of a later *New York Times* article.[39] She posted the video to YouTube and soon added videos about geometry (drawing stars), graph theory (doodling snakes), and prime numbers.

Almost immediately, the videos went viral, gaining over a million views—many from teenage girls, the demographic historically most unlikely to be interested in mathematics.[40] With her video's surging popularity, Vi started earning YouTube advertising revenue, had the aforementioned article

39 Kenneth Chang, "Bending and Stretching Classroom Lessons to Make Math Inspire," *New York Times*, January 17, 2011, http://www.nytimes.com/2011/01/18/science/18prof.html.

40 Ibid.

written about her, and began receiving unsolicited job offers.

Like many bright, creative, ambitious, and ultimately unemployed young graduates, Vi wanted to create a meaningful occupation for herself. And she did—but not by submitting her résumé for "mathemusician" jobs. Instead she dedicated her time to creating little projects that were both fascinating to Vi and useful to others. Many of these projects garnered little attention, but when success struck, it struck big.

When you visit Vi's personal website you'll find it packed with an incredible diversity of projects meant to inform and inspire other people: a blog, podcasts, musical compositions, and instructions for forming balloons into complex geometric shapes.[41]

*   *   *

Think of Vi's style of self-directed learning as a type of operating system: SDL 2.0.

SDL 1.0, the predecessor to SDL 2.0, is the love of learning with which everyone is born. When you teach yourself chess, read novels, dissect insects, learn money management, or discuss philosophy with your friends, you're practicing SDL 1.0. You're certainly doing self-directed learning, but it doesn't necessarily serve anyone but yourself.

In contrast, SDL 2.0 bends self-directed learning toward the needs of others. It begins with your personal interests—such as learning chess, reading novels, or dissecting insects—and then asks, "How can I make this useful to someone else? How can I create value for others?"

When you choose to do ZTC, you also make the choice to

---

41 Explore Vi's projects at http://www.vihart.com.

upgrade your learning to SDL 2.0. Why? Because when you want to leave home and become an economically independent adult, you need to start creating value for other people. That's how you thrive in a market society. When you create value, you identify and serve other people's needs—the basic function of pretty much every business or institution. To get hired, sell your freelance services, start an enterprise, or lead any group of people, you must create value for them. Often "value" will be in the form of money, but don't assume they're synonymous. You can prosper in society without much *money*, but you won't last long if you don't create *value* for other people.

Doing ZTC doesn't mean that everything you do must be for someone else; you can still learn chess, read novels, dissect insects, and do projects that serve only yourself. But it's not enough to just do SDL 1.0. When prioritizing your life, you must begin with the projects that create value for others.[42]

So how do you begin creating value for other people? The simplest way is to work, intern, apprentice, or volunteer for someone. The five young adults who were profiled in "What to Do Instead of College" each took one (or more) of these paths: Tara interned at birth centers, Weezie volunteered at conferences, Sean worked at a bike shop, Brenna apprenticed herself to a master potter, and Allen freelanced.

Some goals don't lend themselves to volunteering, internships, and employment. If you want to learn about art history, for example, then research might take you more quickly to your goal. But to research art history in isolation would create no value for anyone else.

---

42 Steven Pressfield masterfully summarizes this ethic in his book *The War of Art* (New York: Black Irish Entertainment, 2002).

So if you want to make your art-history research useful to other people, what's the solution? The answer is to create a deliverable. A deliverable is any kind of useful product that concretely demonstrates the work you've done. The best deliverables teach, inspire, inform, or entertain; for example, when Vi Hart shared her various projects online, she was creating deliverables. Thus, to share your art-history research, you might:

- create a small website, video, or slide presentation that gives a brief overview of art history and lists the best resources that you found.

- write a blog post or series of Twitter updates narrating your quest.

- offer a one-hour seminar on art history at a library.

Now you've become a purveyor of art history rather than merely a consumer. If these suggestions sound familiar, that's because the previous chapter's assignments offer similar deliverables.

With basic computer literacy, an Internet connection, and a camera or video-recording device, it is possible to create a powerful online deliverable using free technologies and websites. Consider these inexpensive and impactful deliverables:

- **Blog entries:** publish a story about completing an assignment, offer your analysis of a certain event, or create a step-by-step "how-to" post.

- **Photo journal:** take photos during your assignment and publish them with narration.

- **Short video:** record an entertaining, inspiring, and/or instructional video.

- **Website:** create a short article, presentation, or website to share your assignment with the world.

I emphasize digital deliverables because they're cheap, easily shared, fit seamlessly into an online portfolio, and can be used to document most activities. Visit the ZTC website to find examples of high-quality deliverables which you may use to model your own.

Finally, here's a quick note for those lacking self-confidence in their ability to produce a quality deliverable. If you think, "Who am I to write a blog or website? Who would be interested in what I have to say?"—or worse, you hear these messages from family and friends—keep your deliverables private at first. Work hard, solicit feedback from a few people whose judgment you respect (and who respect you), and then revise further before making your deliverables public. Prepare yourself for the inevitable criticism—it's natural, and you shouldn't take it personally. Don't try to please everyone. Take the time to build something that makes you proud, and you'll produce a quality deliverable.

Find Support

Self-directed learning doesn't mean doing everything on your own. Like all people, self-directed learners need support to succeed. This support takes three forms:

1. Peer community

2. Mentorship and guidance

3. Structure and accountability

The third form is typically the biggest challenge for self-directed learners. When Weezie began her gap year, her friends and parents provided ample community and mentorship, but structure and accountability came less easily:

> Taking a semester off (or just time out of school in general) can be daunting for many reasons, particularly the lack of structure. Schools and teachers lay it all out to us from the beginning: the goals, the expectations, what we must do by when, and what resources to use. It's easy to take this sense of structure for granted until you find yourself without it.

Sean described it this way:

> The biggest challenge I face as a self-directed learner/doer-of-things/entrepreneur is the lack of outside structure and accountability. That's a big part of what you pay for when you enroll in college: "Here is what you are expected to do, by these dates. And here are a whole bunch of resources, and a team of people whose job it is to support you."

But other self-directed learners struggle more with finding community or guidance, so we'll look at each of these three forms in turn. As before, an asterisk indicates that further resources may be found at http://www.ztcollege.com.

Finding Peer Community

Let's face it: colleges hold a monopoly over young adult social life. It's difficult to find a concentrated mass of 18- to 25-year olds anywhere else.

Luckily, you don't have to be enrolled in college to be surrounded by a huge group of college-aged peers. You can simply join them: move to a college town, rent a room in an off-campus house,* make friends with your new housemates, hang out with their friends, and go to campus activities, house parties, and other local events. You'll quickly find that not being an official student creates little barrier to participating in college social life. In fact, your nontraditional lifestyle may quickly connect you to the more interesting students.

You may also discover, however, that a "normal" peer group doesn't float your boat. Perhaps your new college friends party too much, aren't motivated enough, or don't inspire you. You may decide to move to a different house or community. Or you may want to start your own student house.

You don't need to own property to start a student house. Convince a handful of your friends to join forces, find a rental house,* pool your resources, and then ask the group's most creditworthy member to sign the lease. Furnish the house with used or inexpensive couches, mattresses, futons, tables, and chairs.* Buy food in bulk, devise a simple and equitable chore system, and focus on doing things together as a house.

Manage the house with a weekly meeting based on a specific, agreed-upon decision-making system.* Host potlucks, discussion nights, game nights, and parties for friends (and perhaps the greater community). Creating a well-run student house is a challenging and rewarding ZTC assignment in and of itself.

Whether you live on your own, with your parents, or in a student house, you can also meet peers through community classes (like dance lessons), themed groups (like knitting circles), or organized programs (like rock climbing).* Working, interning, or volunteering for an organization also provides excellent opportunities. Auditing a college class or sitting in on the big ones is a good way to meet people who are interested in the same subjects as you—just e-mail the professor to ask permission first. Also, some college departments offer evening lectures or colloquia that are free to the public. Find these online or by strolling through campus.

If you're still a teenager, check out Not Back to School Camp (www.nbtsc.org), a summer camp bursting with self-directed teens. Also, browse the ZTC community website and its directory of participants from across the United States and the world.

Finding Mentorship and Guidance

If your learning is self-directed, who will be your "guidance counselor"? Where will you find the mentorship and advice necessary to design your higher education?

Begin with the people who know you best and understand your reasons for choosing an alternative path. These people—whether family members, close friends, or a trusted coach or teacher—will form your first and best advisory panel, cheerleading squad, and sounding board.

Also consider recruiting an outside mentor specifically for the purpose of guiding your self-directed education. Close friends and family can provide excellent positive feedback, but they're often less comfortable providing the critical feedback that facilitates rapid growth. An outside mentor can do this without jeopardizing a preexisting relationship. The strongest outside mentors:

- have done or are currently doing the things that you want to do (or possess the character traits that you wish to possess);

- can observe your performance in the areas in which you need improvement; and

- can remain objective whether you succeed or fail; this is why team members and bosses, who are directly invested in your performance, may not make the best mentors.

Where do you find an outside mentor? If you know exactly which industry you want to break into (e.g., wilderness photography, coffee importing, or social media) then you can seek an industry-specific mentor. Volunteering, interning, or working for someone is a solid way to establish this connection, although it's best to solicit mentorship only after you are no longer working together. Some social networking websites (most notably LinkedIn) offer more formal opportunities to introduce yourself to a highly qualified professional.* And you can always begin by asking your network-at-large if anyone knows somebody who works in your field of interest. Many adults would love to mentor or provide one-time advice to a curious self-directed learner, but they don't advertise it. You've got to seek them out.

What if you don't know exactly where you'd like to go with your self-directed higher education? Then you'll need a mentor who's experienced more generally in self-directed learning and entrepreneurship. Ideally this person will help you connect with industry-specific mentors while also helping you design your broader personal curriculum. It can be hard to find this combination of skills in a mentor, which is another reason I created the online ZTC community. On the website, you can find experienced mentors who understand the ZTC vision and are excited to offer their services to self-directed young people.

In addition to that general guidance, self-directed learners often need one-time help with specific hurdles. How do I begin selling my art online? How do I plan a bike trip across the United States? Who can recommend the top books on archaeology? How can I improve my writing? You can easily find the names of potentially helpful individuals by reading books, searching online, and probing your social network. But how do you get them to actually help you?

Here's a simple blueprint for making contact with any potential advisor. After you find the prospective person:

1. Determine the specific task you'd like their help in achieving. Ideally, the task will be a small step in a larger ZTC assignment.

2. Call, e-mail, or, in the case of a college professor, knock on that person's door during office hours.

3. Briefly introduce yourself and explain the self-directed

assignment that you're pursuing. Then, without beat-
ing around the bush, directly request their assistance
with the specific step that's troubling you. The entire
call/e-mail/conversation doesn't need to take more
than a minute—if it's significantly longer, you're
unwittingly demonstrating that you don't respect the
person's time. (Of course, if the other person is highly
engaged in the conversation, it can go longer!)

4. If you're rejected, ask the person to point you in the
   direction of another person or organization that
   might be able to help.

Succeeding as a self-directed learner inevitably means cul-
tivating your willingness and ability to approach strangers
and ask for what you need. I'll illustrate this with two personal stories.

In 2010 I ran a leadership retreat centered on the challenge
of approaching strangers and asking for help. My group of
seven teenage unschoolers descended on the small, bustling
town of Ashland, Oregon, and they walked around for two
weeks, boldly asking residents for the opportunity to interview, shadow, intern, volunteer for, or simply chat with them.
Each day the assignment was the same: start with clear goals
("I want to explore the field of child psychology" or "I want
to see the inside of a professional theater"), find the locals
who might be able to help, and approach them. None of these
teens started with exceptional social skills, but by the end of
the program, they felt empowered to return home and begin
self-directing their lives. When you spend enough time asking
strangers for help, you stop fearing rejection.

Earlier, in 2008, I interviewed to be a trip leader with a

gap-year company that runs trips to South America. My credentials were strong: I spoke Spanish, I'd traveled across the continent, I was a Wilderness First Responder and Emergency Medical Technician, and I had multiple years of experience in outdoor program management. The in-person interview went well. But a month later I learned that I didn't make the cut; apparently there had been 150 applicants for two spots.

While waiting to hear about the job, however, I had become convinced that leading extended international trips perfectly fit my interests and abilities. So when I wasn't hired, I decided that I'd just organize a trip myself.

Through my work at Not Back to School Camp, I already knew that many unschoolers were interested in world travel and wanted more opportunities to connect with each other. I e-mailed the owner of the company that had rejected me and wrote (in so many words), "Hey, I'd like to organize my own trip to South America. Can you help me figure out the legal stuff?" Expecting some sort of "We're not going to help our competition!" response, I was delighted when he offered his assistance. One month later my little travel company, Unschool Adventures, was born, and four months later I found myself getting paid to backpack around Argentina with a group of eight teenagers.

Again, the principle is: when you spend enough time asking strangers for help, you stop fearing rejection.

Remember, though, that asking for mentorship is always an exchange. If you meet with someone and expect to simply extract information, the relationship won't last long. Your potential mentor owes you nothing, so create value in every exchange. Give something to everyone who helps you. Invite them out for a cup of coffee or tea—your treat. If your mentors are highly talented or highly busy, pay them an hourly rate or barter your skills (web design, landscaping, etc.) in exchange for their time. And sometimes a friendly smile, respect, and a willingness to listen might be payment enough.

Finally, a small but important issue: when introducing yourself to potential mentors who aren't familiar with the concept of ZTC, what do you call yourself? Using the terms "unschooler," "uncolleger," "autodidact," or "self-directed learner" inevitably leaves people with confused looks on their faces. My suggestions:

- Say that you're taking a gap year to get some real-life experience before making your college decision.

- Say that you're pursuing a combination of internships and independent research as an alternative to college.

- Say that you're doing an independent study as part of an experimental, unaccredited, tuition-free college. Send them to the ZTC website if they're curious.

Finding Structure and Accountability

How do you keep yourself accountable to your self-directed goals without college professors, guidance counselors, and other authorities? This may be the biggest challenge you face as a self-directed learner.

The easiest place to find such structure is with the mentors and guides you've recruited. In addition to providing guidance for your ZTC assignments, these people can double as enforcers of accountability. A life coach or wide-focus mentor like those found in the online ZTC directory can work with you to schedule goals and overcome personal blocks.

But whether or not you recruit a mentor, you can start creating your own structure by writing a syllabus, curriculum, or goal list. Weezie described how she began:

> The first thing I did, about a week after deciding to not return for the spring semester of my school, was to create my own syllabus for the semester. Although it has been tweaked and modified in various ways, the basic gist of it has been incredibly helpful in focusing myself amidst the many options of things to do.

Earlier, I mentioned the idea of creating such a list, and it's a good place to start. But there's a problem with writing ambitious goal lists: we often tuck them away and forget them, or we deliberately ignore them. Such is human nature. Much of the power of a personal goal list, then, comes not from the list itself but rather from your public acknowledgment of it.

StickK.com embraces this idea by enabling people to create online "Commitment Contracts." You start by entering a specific goal and time frame for completing it. Then you have the chance to put money on the line. If you complete the goal, you keep your money; if you fail, you lose it. The money either goes to a designated individual (like a friend), a good charity (one that you believe in), or an "anti-charity" (one that you don't believe in). To monitor this process, stickK asks you to nominate a referee who can verify whether you have completed your goal. The website also includes social media tools so you can spread word of your wager.[43]

This kind of high-pressure, high-visibility goal setting

---

43 StickK.com, accessed December 1, 2011.

may not be your cup of tea, but it's worth recognizing the key elements:

- Put your reputation or money on the line.

- Enlist a trusted "referee" to monitor your progress.

- Publicly announce your goal.

A lower-octane version of the stickK strategy is to form an "accountability partnership."* Tara explained the idea to me this way:

> As self-directed learners, together we must be our own professors, bosses, and enthusiasts. This is exciting! However, it's often difficult to remain afloat amongst a raging sea of ideas and dreams. This is where your accountability partner comes in.
>
> Accountability partners set goals together, create deadlines for each other's projects, and communicate regularly to keep on track. Find someone who will challenge, encourage, and inspire you, and for whom you can do the same in turn (without being afraid of sharing your crappiest work). This can be in-person, online, or via phone. I highly recommended keeping written records of your meetings.

Tara started her first accountability partnership by creating an outline of her current projects and goals, which included writing a book, starting a business, and saving money for an international adventure. Her partner, Jessica (a fellow self-directed learner), did the same. Every two weeks, Tara and Jessica recorded their progress and e-mailed their outlines to each other. To provide evidence of their progress, they attached samples of their notes, preparatory work, and deliverables. They then spoke on the phone for an hour to review each other's outlines, ask questions, provide feedback, and help the other person talk through challenges and find resources. They finished the meeting by stating the goals that they would accomplish in the next two weeks.

*   *   *

Finding support in the forms of peer community, mentorship, and systems of accountability may be the greatest challenge you face as a self-directed learner, and perhaps it's the reason that many young people see no alternative to college. But a college degree doesn't solve this challenge either. Successful adults must always seek out communities that nourish them, mentors who inspire them, and systems of structure and accountability that work for them. Choosing the ZTC path simply means developing these skills starting now, rather than four years down the line.

Market Yourself

When an employer looks at a résumé and sees a college degree, she automatically assumes that the applicant:

- is reasonably intelligent,

- has a strong work ethic,

- possesses certain broad skills (critical reading, writing, problem-solving, etc.), and

- possesses certain specific skills (those indicated by the applicant's major).

Economists would call this the "signaling" function of the college degree. Sending such a signal to your future employers, financial backers, and project partners is important, but, as marketer Seth Godin explains, a powerful signal need not come from an expensive institution:

> Does a $40,000 a year education that comes with an elite degree deliver ten times the education of a cheaper but no less rigorous self-generated approach assembled from less famous institutions and free or inexpensive resources? . . . What would happen if people spent [the money] building up a work history instead? On becoming smarter, more flexible, more self-sufficient and yes, able to take more risk because they owe less money . . . ?
>
> There's no doubt that we need smarter and more motivated

people in our organizations. I'm not sure we need them to be better labeled or more accredited.[44]

You don't need a fancy label or accreditation attached to your name, but, to skip college successfully, you *will* need to create your own signal. The best way to begin doing this is to build a high-quality online portfolio that vividly demonstrates your intelligence, work ethic, and skills.

But a high-quality portfolio is not enough to automatically generate work, just as a college degree won't automatically bring employers knocking. After creating your signal, you must also get the right eyes to see it. Therefore, "marketing yourself" in Zero Tuition College means both creating a compelling portfolio and making sure the right people know that it exists.

The ZTC strategy largely integrates both of those tasks already. By doing assignments and creating deliverables, you generate a wealth of portfolio material. By seeking support from mentors, peers, professionals, and fellow travelers, you build an audience. Creating a portfolio and spreading the word will follow naturally.

Can this path really replace the branding power of a college degree? There are no guarantees, of course, but remember that, by making a cost-efficient decision against going to college and choosing to blaze your own path, you'll demonstrate initiative, courage, intelligence, independence, financial awareness, and a host of other vital attributes. Yes,

---

44 Seth Godin, "Buying an Education or Buying a Brand?" *Seth Godin's Blog*, April 15, 2011, http://sethgodin.typepad.com/seths_blog/2011/04/buying-an-education-or-buying-a-brand.html.

you'll often need to explain your alternative path to employers or other gatekeepers; yes, you may need to use clever tactics to get their attention. But as you do these things, you will further build your unique portfolio and story.

Building Your Portfolio

What elements go into a strong online portfolio? On the ZTC website, you'll find examples of high-quality portfolios from both self-directed learners and the traditionally educated. Their most common elements include:

- Blog: short updates from projects, work, or adventures

- Writing: articles, essays, or opinion pieces which are longer and/or more formal than blogs

- Multimedia: photos, videos, music, illustrations, slideshow presentations, etc.

- Syllabus or goal list: a list of projects, assignments, and goals

- Bio: a short story explaining who they are and why they chose an alternative path

- Résumé or curriculum vitae: a formal, chronological record of education (including nontraditional education) and work history

- Testimonials and letters of recommendation: short, compelling statements from mentors, clients, employers, or coworkers

- Business services (if applicable): a description of current products or services, profiles of former clients, and a call to action (e.g., "hire me," "get a free sample," or "request a quote")

- Social media: links to profiles on LinkedIn, Facebook, Twitter, etc.

- Contact information: an obvious and easy way to get in touch

Choose your own elements carefully. You can design a strong portfolio without a blog or testimonials, but if your portfolio lacks a bio or easy-to-find contact information, visitors will quickly leave your site or ignore the services that you offer. Search online for examples in your specific field. A photographer's portfolio (multimedia-heavy) won't look like a public intellectual's portfolio (writing-heavy), while a freelance carpenter's portfolio (business- and testimonial-heavy) won't look like a world traveler's portfolio (blog- and social media-heavy). Figure out which elements are utilized in the most compelling portfolios in your field, then mimic, polish, get feedback, and repeat.

This chapter doesn't provide a comprehensive overview of online portfolio design techniques; the best place to find that is online. However, here are a few core principles that I recommend you stick to:

- Design a portfolio that emphasizes your work and value creation. Highly personal status updates, ramblings, and photos of your pets don't belong on a professional portfolio.

- Make the portfolio simple, clean, and easy to use. Could your grandma navigate the site and quickly find the most important content?

- Showcase your best work, biggest projects, grandest plans, most polished deliverables, and most enthusiastic testimonials—but don't deceive. Focusing on your top achievements never means lying to make yourself look better.

If you highlight only your successes, you sometimes leave out the most interesting parts of your story. Recognizing this, Tina Seelig, director of the Stanford Technology Ventures Program at Stanford University, suggests that budding entrepreneurs also create a "failure résumé" in addition to a normal résumé.[45]

A failure résumé highlights your struggles and miscalculations rather than just your successes. For example, a failure résumé entry may read: "June-August 2012: attempted to bike across Europe and volunteer at small farms along the way; ran out of money halfway. Plan to return next year." Briefly describe the risks you took, the things you learned, and, if applicable, your plans to change or revisit this goal in the future. This isn't a place to mention really terrible mistakes ("Got a DUI!"); it's an opportunity to demonstrate honesty, strength, resilience, and the entrepreneurial ethic of embracing risk. In my own portfolio, I combine my goal list with my

---

45 Tina Seelig, "Learning From Failure," Stanford Entrepreneurial Thought Leader Speaker Series podcast, 00:44, April 12, 2006, http://ecorner.stanford.edu/authorMaterialInfo.html?mid=1469.

failure résumé so that visitors get a realistic impression of my life: a healthy mixture of both successes and failures.[46]

How should you design and host your portfolio? If you're a web guru (or know one), create your portfolio from scratch. For everyone else, find a portfolio-building website that offers eye-catching templates and easy instructions for adding writing, multimedia, a syllabus, links, a blog, etc.* The best portfolio-building sites charge a small monthly fee and provide a much higher level of professionalism than the free sites.

Whether you build your own portfolio or use a portfolio-building site, make sure to pay the nominal fee for a personally branded domain (i.e., www.yourname.com, www.yourbusiness.com, or www.yourclevertitle.com). Nothing kills a portfolio's professional image faster than a web address like "mike155.wordpress.com."

Spreading the Word

Once you've built your portfolio, you need to figure out who will read it and where they'll come from. To begin, imagine three concentric circles: one small, one medium, and one large.

The small circle encompasses your loyal friends, family, and closest associates. These people support you unconditionally, tell their friends about you, and are convinced that you're pretty much the greatest thing since sliced bread. Call these people your "true fans."[47]

---

46 See it at www.blakeboles.com.

47 This definition of "true fans" comes from author Kevin Kelly, "1,000 True Fans," *The Technium*, March 4, 2008, http://www.kk.org/thetechnium/archives/2008/03/1000_true_fans.php.

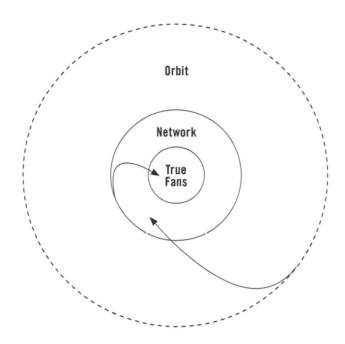

The medium circle encompasses the people with whom you have positively interacted, such as previous clients, readers of your blog, or people you connected with at an event. These people know about you and your work, but only in a limited way. Call these people your "network."

The large circle—much larger than the other two—consists of the wide world of strangers who might benefit from your work but don't know you. Call these people your "orbit."

As discussed above, marketing yourself begins with building a strong portfolio that demonstrates the value that you've created. However, only your true fans know about that value, although your network might be peripherally aware. The goal of marketing yourself is to draw people into progressively smaller circles, to turn your orbit into your network, and your network into true fans.

Please note that I'm not talking about becoming some kind of smarmy, self-promoting huckster. I'm simply talking about increasing the number of people to whom you provide value.

So how do you do this? The answer is simple yet challenging: find the people who struggle with a problem that you understand, and then make their lives easier.

Don't hand out business cards indiscriminately. Don't hard sell. Don't spam. To market yourself, give other people your time, focus, and presence. If you do—and do it well—they'll ask for your card, portfolio, or hourly rate, tell their friends about you, and migrate into your smaller circles.

There are two steps to this process. First, you have to find people whose problems you understand, and then you need to make their lives easier. What might this look like?

- Show up at a local business, studio, or nonprofit. Explain your background and interest in what they do, and then ask how you can help out—no task too small—while learning along the way. When they ask about your qualifications, point them to your portfolio. If no opportunities exist, ask if they know someone else who might need your help.

- Attend a conference or other event where your community of interest gathers. (If you can't afford a ticket, volunteer your services in exchange for entry.) Turn on your extroverted side: drink coffee, go with a friend, or do whatever else you need to do to become a social butterfly. Smile, introduce yourself, ask good questions, and listen to other people's stories twice as often as you tell your own. When you run into someone you can genuinely help or connect somehow, offer to do so without asking for anything in return. Exchange contact information and then be the first to touch base when you get home. Follow through on what you promise.

- Search for people who are tackling the same problems as you are but who are at a lower skill level. If you blog, seek out new bloggers writing about your same topic. If you design jewelry, find other jewelers in your region. Then e-mail them and offer to help. For a blogger, this might mean promoting their writing on your site or authoring a guest post. For a jewelry designer, this might mean sending a few sample pieces that demonstrate a certain technique you've mastered but they're still struggling with. Put yourself in the other person's shoes and ask yourself what would have really helped you at this point in your development.

- Connect two people who will benefit from knowing each other. Tell a new acquaintance about an interesting job opening. Introduce friends who are working on similar problems. Link someone in your network to a person, organization, or product that will make his life easier.

- Mentor someone seeking guidance in your field of expertise. (The ZTC community website offers many potential mentees.)

- Post links online to the best writing, media, and other content you find. Create an e-mail newsletter that offers this same content to make it handy for people who don't constantly check their social media accounts.

Basically, the best way to market yourself is to do good things for people whose problems you understand, without much regard for what you get in return.

A few other principles hold constant. Think of every marketing encounter as a trade of your time and energy for someone else's time and energy. Always be the person giving more. Never ask for someone else's time or money for free. That's the surest path to receiving nothing at all.

Every successful marketing encounter also requires deep listening. You can find good books on how to practice deep listening,* but here's the gist: Imagine a little person in your head, sitting on a chair, reading a book. That's your mind. Deep listening means telling the little person in your head to put the book down so that you can actually pay attention to the needs and concerns of others. Without this skill you'll make a crappy entrepreneur, employee, mentor, or value-creator of any kind.

Finally, make sure that you're easy to find. Add an automatic signature to your e-mails with your phone, e-mail address, and portfolio website address. When you meet someone incredible, be sure to give them your contact information. Ensure that people can easily find you at the golden moment when they, remembering the good things you've done for them, have a valuable new opportunity for you.

Getting Your Foot in the Door

"The kind of marketing that you're describing might make me look good and feel magnanimous," you may think, "but will it really help me get hired?" Can you actually get a job simply by doing self-directed assignments, creating deliverables, making a portfolio, and doing nice things for people in need?

Well, yes.

The ZTC marketing approach makes a calculated exchange: it trades traditional, through-the-front-door hiring power (in the form of big-name college branding) for non-traditional, through-the-back-door hiring power. Whereas a traditional résumé may get you past the human resources department, ZTC skips HR entirely by focusing on the power of internal referrals.

An internal referral is when a current employee suggests you as a potential hire. Today, a significant amount of hiring is done this way.[48] Not only does a referral save the company the time and expense of recruiting, but it also helps match a candidate to the company's culture—a factor difficult to judge from a résumé.

In 2011, a technology blog explained how to get hired by Apple, one of the most coveted employers in Silicon Valley:

> Get a referral. It's easier than it sounds, and getting your-self talent-spotted is often a direct route into the Cupertino campus. . . . Apple staff are usually happy to recommend newbies for upcoming jobs (as long as you have the relevant experience and skills, of course). . . .
>
> [I]f you're a "known entity" rather than a CV crossing a recruiter's desk, you'll get an easier ride. No practical tests at

---

48 According to 2010 data, 69% of employers say they have a formal employee referral program, and 26% of external hires are generated from employee referrals, making referrals the main source of hire. "Referral Madness: How Employee Referral Programs Turn Good Employees into Great Recruiters and Grow Your Bottom Line," CareerBuilder, accessed January 27, 2012, http://www.careerbuildercommunications.com/pdf/referralbook.pdf?sc_cmp2=JP_RSC_Report_Referral.

the interview stage, no intense interview, and more team intro-
ductions than interviewer inquisitions.[49]

Let's assume that you don't know someone at Apple. How
can you garner an internal referral? The blog author suggests introducing yourself to an employee (not necessarily a
department manager) through a professional social networking website, getting an internship, creating a killer app, or
answering questions in the Apple support forum.

Some people take more creative paths to an internal referral. The blog author also mentions the story of a notorious
hacker who was awarded an Apple internship after cracking
every new iPhone operating system that was released.

And in *The Education of Millionaires*, author Michael
Ellsberg relates the story of Marian Schembari, a liberal arts
college graduate trying to break into the New York publishing industry. After sending her highly polished résumé and
customized cover letters to almost every publishing house in
New York and receiving no response, Marian took a different approach. She purchased $100 worth of Facebook ads
with the title, "I want to work for HarperCollins," and tar-
geted the ads to appear for employees of six major publishing
houses. A HarperCollins executive saw the ad and blogged
about it, and Marian's story soon spread throughout the publishing industry. Marian received e-mail from each of the six
publishing houses and eventually took an entry-level position
with a major New York literary public relations firm.[50]

These tactics don't just apply to entry-level positions. In

49 James Holland, "How to Get a Job at Apple," Electricpig, February 4, 2011,
    http://www.electricpig.co.uk/2011/02/04/how-to-get-a-job-at-apple.
50 Ellsberg, *Education of Millionaires*, 175–77.

2009, Alec Brownstein, a 28-year-old advertising copywriter, wanted to find a better employer. While googling the creative directors for whom he would have loved to work, Alec noticed that no sponsored links appeared next to their names. Alec realized that these creative directors probably googled themselves "embarrassingly frequently" (as he himself did), so Alec purchased the ad space. Now whenever someone searched Google for one of the creative director's names, this message appeared on the top of the page, followed by a link to Alec's portfolio website:

> "Hey, [creative director's name]: Goooogling yourself is a lot of fun. Hiring me is fun, too."

Over the next few months, all but one of the creative directors called Alec, and two of them offered him a job. The total cost of Alec's campaign: six dollars.[51]

* * *

Getting your foot in the door for a job always begins with possessing the right skills, knowledge, and background. Self-directed learners build these qualities with the assignments they give themselves, the feedback they solicit, the deliverables they create, and the portfolios they compile. Then, by helping others in need (and occasionally devising a clever way to get noticed), they connect with the right person, who can provide them with an internal referral.

---

51 Lauren Idvik, "How To: Land Your Dream Job Using Google AdWords," Mashable Business, May 13, 2010, http://mashable.com/2010/05/13/job-google-ad-words.

Doing Zero Tuition College doesn't reduce your hiring potential in the modern job market—it simply changes your trajectory. Why compete with droves of college graduates trying to push their way through the front door when someone can wave you through the back?

Finding My Unschool Adventures

When I graduated from my self-directed college program, I asked myself the three ZTC self-knowledge questions. Here's what I discovered:

- Were I to die in a year, I would spend as much time as I could working with young people, being outside, adventuring with friends, visiting family, and traveling.

- To change the world within three years, I would create some new type of summer camp, alternative school, or experiential education program.

- If amassing long-term wealth were impossible, then I would focus on filling my life with memorable experiences and meaningful relationships, remaining independent, and staying out of debt.

I began by jumping into the California outdoor education industry, through which I took groups of fifth graders for hikes, taught them basic science, and led them across high-ropes courses. Every day I worked in some new pristine wilderness. The room-and-board-compensated jobs left me with a few thousand dollars in the bank each month, and, without student loan debt, my finances were in the black from the beginning.

Between outdoor education jobs, I tried my hand at food service and teaching gigs. While spending a winter doing market research for Heavenly (a ski resort where I snowboarded across the mountain and interviewed guests on chairlifts), I took evening classes to get trained as an Emergency Medical Technician and took a week off to become a Wilderness First Responder. Using these credentials, I worked each summer at my childhood summer camp as the assistant director and, later, acting director, teaching windsurfing and leading backpacking trips. None of these jobs or opportunities demanded a college degree; my previous experience and the occasional internal referral got me hired. Without a lease to my name, I was able to save enough money from seasonal jobs to hike 500 miles on the Pacific Crest Trail, spend three months backpacking across South America, and visit family often.

Eventually I got fed up working for other people, so I started looking for opportunities to start my own camp/school/program. The teen unschoolers from Not Back to School Camp (where I had been working for a few summers) hungered for travel and bonding opportunities, so I organized a six-week trip to Argentina. Our little group spent two weeks taking Spanish classes in the Andean foothills, two weeks learning tango in Buenos Aires, and two weeks during which the teens planned the itinerary, managed the budget, and traveled where they wished. I returned stateside with a paycheck and plenty of new ideas for Unschool Adventures. The next year I led a writing retreat in which 20 unschoolers converged on an Oregon beach house for a month to write their own novels, and this was followed by two teen leadership programs and trips to Australia and South America.

By 26 I was getting paid to travel the world, working with teen unschoolers, and leaving myself enough time and money to visit friends and family, live comfortably, write often, and read constantly. My first book, *College Without High School*, was en route to the publisher. Life was good.

That's the rosy version of the story, of course. Between successes I had my share of failures and personal crises, like when I freaked out after my first week of teaching snowboarding, quit without notice, and drove the length of California and back to clear my mind. Or when I left a few of my outdoor-education jobs early, burning bridges with bosses and coworkers I inevitably encountered later. Or when I spent all my savings to move to Portland, sit alone in my little apartment, experience the misery of online dating, start and abandon a new company (wasting dozens of people's time in the process), and spend far more time in Powell's Books than any healthy human should.

But when the dust settled from my messy, self-directed journey, I realized that I had stayed true to my ZTC intentions. I had enjoyed life enough to hedge against the die-in-one-year scenario while also gaining the experience necessary to start a company and publish a book. I enjoyed strong relationships with friends and family, lived free of debt, and chose when I woke up every day. I was poor by Western standards but wealthy by the standard of human needs, both tangible and intangible. Many people helped me along this path, but one thing never helped: the belief that a traditional education was all that you needed for success.

For some, the urge to direct their own lives strikes like lightning. For others, it slowly overwhelms. No matter how this message arrives, act upon it. There is always life beyond the expected path.

14 WAYS TO START YOUR JOURNEY

1. Find and interview three people who have chosen to skip college. If you don't know anyone, browse the online community at http://www.ztcollege.com. Set up a meeting or send them a short e-mail with a few questions about the parts of skipping college that most intimidate you. Find out which books, people, communities, strategies, and other resources helped them succeed.

2. If you're currently in college or will be soon, speak with someone in the admissions department to figure out your options for taking time off. Can you take a leave of absence? Can you defer your enrollment? Explain that you're considering a gap year—admissions people understand that language.

3. Read *The Teenage Liberation Handbook*, Grace Llewellyn's powerful and inspirational introduction to the educational philosophy of unschooling.

4. Spend an evening with the three questions from the chapter about self-knowledge. Take them seriously— this is your life we're talking about! Write down a list of 50 potential goals (both short-term and long-term) that excite you so much that your fingers can't type fast enough.

5. Create your first Zero Tuition College assignment, ensuring that it is as concrete as possible. Then write down a list of three "baby steps" that will lead you toward your goal. You should be able to complete the

first step within five minutes of finishing your list, the second within a day, and the third within a week. For example, if my assignment were to "live and work in New Zealand for three months, couchsurfing and using volunteering sites to spend less than $500 per month," then my baby steps might look like:

- Create an account on CouchSurfing.org.

- Research the cost of living in various parts of New Zealand.

- Using information from travel guides and blogs, draft an anticipated monthly budget.

Create online calendar alerts and, more importantly, ask a friend to follow up with you to ensure that you complete the steps.

6. Create and publish one deliverable that tells the story of something you've already done: write a blog post, upload a video, or share a set of photos or piece of artwork. Tell your friends about the deliverable via social media and e-mail.

7. E-mail one professional whose work you admire. Briefly introduce yourself and mention two or three specific things that you love about his or her work. Ask one focused question that wouldn't necessarily require more than a minute to answer but could potentially spark a larger conversation.

8. To prove to yourself that you can meet interesting peers without a college ID, attend a community

event like a dance class or open mic. Alternatively, go to a college campus event that seems like it's only for students, but nothing explicitly prohibits non-students from attending. Introduce yourself to one interesting-looking person. Bonus points if you ask him or her out for coffee.

9. Drop in on the office hours of a college professor or graduate student (the times are often posted online) and ask her what it takes to excel in her field. If asked about your student status, explain that you're taking a gap year to investigate your options.

10. Create an accountability partnership by following the advice in the "Find Support" chapter. Use this partnership to achieve a small goal that you've been struggling with for a long time.

11. Write a failure résumé that highlights your biggest gambles, overreaches, and mistakes—and what you learned from them.

12. Begin building your portfolio. Using a portfolio-building website (suggestions available on http://www.ztcollege.com), choose a design that matches your taste, and immediately add a bio, syllabus, and contact information. Figure out how to obtain a personally branded domain name (most portfolio sites make this easy).

13. Do something good for a person whose problem you understand. Follow one of the concrete suggestions

from the "Spreading the Word" section of "Market Yourself."

14. Remember that the self-directed learners profiled in this book are just examples. If you feel nowhere near as cool or capable as they seem, that's okay. The ultimate goal behind ZTC is to challenge yourself, grow, find happiness, and build self-knowledge. You can do this your own way. Begin today.

INSPIRATION FOR THE ROAD AHEAD

Many talented people have thought about the same problems that inspired Zero Tuition College far longer than I have. On your self-directed journey, I highly recommend looking up the following people and reading (or listening to) what they have to say. Some of these people don't necessarily espouse skipping college, but all of them support purposeful, self-directed learning at the college level.

Daniel Pink

Business writer Daniel Pink's first book, *Free Agent Nation*, was the first to really advocate for unschooling as a form of entrepreneurial education. All of Pink's writings deserve your time, but his 2009 *Drive* tops the list. In it, he writes:

> In environments where extrinsic rewards are most salient, many people work only to the point that triggers [a] reward—and no further. So if students get a prize for reading three books, many won't pick up a fourth, let alone embark on a lifetime of reading—just as executives who hit their quarterly numbers often won't boost earnings a penny more, let alone contemplate the long-term health of their company. . . . Greatness and nearsightedness are incompatible. Meaningful achievement depends on lifting one's sights and pushing toward the horizon.[52]

---

52 Pink, *Drive*, 56–57.

Tina Seelig

As director of the Stanford Technology Ventures Program, Tina Seelig may be responsible for kindling more creativity in young minds than any other higher-education professional. Her book and online video series, *What I Wish I Knew When I Was 20*, explains:

> The typical classroom has a teacher who views his or her job as pouring information. . . . This couldn't be any more different from life after college, where you are your own teacher, charged with figuring out what you need to know, where to find the information, and how to absorb it. In fact, real life is the ultimate open book exam. The doors are thrown wide open, allowing you to draw on endless resources around you as you tackle open-ended problems related to work, family, friends, and the world at large.[53]

John Taylor Gatto

John Taylor Gatto was the man who first inspired me (and many others) down the path of alternative education. In 2010, I accomplished one of my life goals—to have a beer with him. Pick up his 2010 *Weapons of Mass Instruction* to find razor-sharp analyses like this:

> Where you go to college, or even if you go at all, only makes a difference if you believe the spell that has been put on you. Is it money you want? In an hour from where you live I could take

---

53 Tina Seelig, *What I Wish I Knew When I Was 20: A Crash Course on Making Your Place in the World* (New York: HarperCollins, 2009), 11–13. To find Seelig's online video series—as well as a wealth of other material—visit her website at http://ecorner.stanford.edu/author/tina_seelig.

you to a common hot dog vendor who makes more of that than the mayor of New York and the president of the United States combined; is it being of real use to society?—become a pet sitter so that people can take vacations without abusing their critters. Like voodoo, where you go to college—or even if you go at all—is only a real question in minds bewildered by illusion.

That's not to say that education doesn't matter. It does. You need finely tuned critical judgment to defend yourself in the dangerous house of mirrors America has become. It's just that college won't give you education. Only you can do that.[54]

Matthew Crawford

A practicing motorcycle mechanic with a PhD in political philosophy, Matthew Crawford argues convincingly against office-based "knowledge work" and in favor of the pleasure (and economic security) of working with one's hands. From his 2010 book, *Shop Class as Soulcraft*:

When you do the math problems at the back of the chapter in an algebra textbook, you are problem solving. If the chapter is entitled "Systems of two equations with two unknowns," you know exactly which methods to use. In such a constrained situation, the pertinent context in which to view the problem has already been determined, so there is no effort of interpretation required. But in the real world, problems don't present themselves in this predigested way; usually there is too much information, and it is difficult to know what is pertinent and what isn't. . . . [A solution]

---

54 John Taylor Gatto, *Weapons of Mass Instruction: A Schoolteacher's Journey through the Dark World of Compulsory Schooling*, (Gabriola Island: New Society Publishers, 2009), 160–61.

cannot be achieved by the application of rules, and requires the kind of judgment that comes with experience. The value and job security of the mechanic lie in the fact that he has this firsthand, personal knowledge.[55]

Paul Graham

Silicon Valley programmer and venture capitalist Paul Graham writes poignant essays, which he shares on his website, PaulGraham.com. From my favorite one, which was intended for a high school graduation:

> The best protection is always to be working on hard problems. Writing novels is hard. Reading novels isn't. Hard means worry: if you're not worrying that something you're making will come out badly, or that you won't be able to understand something you're studying, then it isn't hard enough.[56]

William Deresiewicz

A former Yale English professor, Deresiewicz wrote two seminal articles critiquing traditional education, "The Disadvantages of an Elite Education" and "Solitude and Leadership." From the former:

> When parents explain why they work so hard to give their children the best possible education, they invariably say it is because of the opportunities it opens up. But what of the opportunities it

---

55 Crawford, *Shop Class as Soulcraft*, 35–36.

56 Paul Graham, "What You'll Wish You'd Known," January 2005, http://www. paulgraham.com/hs.html.

shuts down? An elite education gives you the chance to be rich—which is, after all, what we're talking about—but it takes away the chance not to be. Yet the opportunity not to be rich is one of the greatest opportunities with which young Americans have been blessed. . . . You can live comfortably in the United States as a schoolteacher, or a community organizer, or a civil rights lawyer, or an artist—that is, by any reasonable definition of comfort. You have to live in an ordinary house instead of an apartment in Manhattan or a mansion in L.A. . . . [B]ut what are such losses when set against the opportunity to do work you believe in, work you're suited for, work you love, every day of your life?[57]

Seth Godin

The bald-headed guru of modern marketing, Seth Godin has long questioned the power of college-for-all. Don't miss his blog posts entitled "Buying an education or buying a brand?," "Why bother having a resume?," and "The coming melt-down in higher education (as seen by a marketer)." In the last he writes:

[T]here are tons of ways to get a cheap, liberal education, one that exposes you to the world, permits you to have significant interactions with people who matter and to learn to make a difference. . . . Most of these ways, though, aren't heavily marketed nor do they involve going to a tradition-steeped two-hundred-year old institution with a wrestling team. Things like gap years, research internships and entrepreneurial or social ventures afte

---

57 William Deresiewicz, "The Disadvantages of an Elite Education," *The American Scholar*, Summer 2008, accessed March 7, 2012, http://theamerican scholar.org/the-disadvantages-of-an-elite-education.

high school are opening doors for students who are eager to discover the new.[58]

Anya Kamenetz

In 2009, Anya Kamenetz heralded the end of college as we know it with her book *DIY U*. But you may want to focus on her free 2011 e-book, *The Edupunks' Guide to a DIY Credential*, which offers ZTC-style guidance and excellent links to online learning resources.[59] Here she talks about the impacts of free resources like TED Talks on the future of higher education:

> [I]f you were starting a top university today, what would it look like? You would start by gathering the very best minds from around the world, from every discipline. Since we're living in an age of abundant, not scarce, information, you'd curate the lectures carefully, with a focus on the new and original, rather than offer a course on every possible topic. You'd create a sustainable economic model by focusing on technological rather than physical infrastructure, and by getting people of means to pay for a specialized experience. You'd also construct a robust network so people could access resources whenever and from wherever they

---

58 Seth Godin, "The Coming Melt-Down in Higher Education (as Seen by a Marketer)," April 29, 2010, http://sethgodin.typepad.com/seths_blog/2010/04/the-coming-meltdown-in-higher-education-as-seen-by-a-marketer.html. Also, don't miss his free compilation of education-related essays, *Stop Stealing Dreams*.

59 To download the book, go to http://edupunksguide.org.

like, and you'd give them the tools to collaborate beyond the lecture hall. . . . If you did all that, well, you'd have TED.[60]

Peter Thiel

PayPal cofounder, hedge fund manager, and venture capitalist Peter Thiel has long questioned the value of higher education—and then he put his money where his mouth is. In 2010 Thiel called higher education a "bubble" and gave 20 ambitious young adults $100,000 each to drop out of college for two years and start a company.[61] In an interview with TechCrunch, Thiel explained:

> Education may be the only thing people still believe in in the United States. To question education is really dangerous. It is the absolute taboo. It's like telling the world there's no Santa Claus. . . .
>
> If Harvard were really the best education, if it makes that much of a difference, why not franchise it so more people can attend? Why not create 100 Harvard affiliates? . . . It's something about the scarcity and the status. In education your value depends on other people failing.[62]

---

60 Anya Kamenetz, "How TED Connects the Idea-Hungry Elite," *Fast Company*, September 1, 2010, http://www.fastcompany.com/magazine/148/how-ted-became-the-new-harvard.html.

61 For more information, visit http://www.thielfellowship.org.

62 Sarah Lacy, "Peter Thiel: We're in a Bubble and It's Not the Internet. It's Higher Education," *TechCrunch*, April 10, 2011, http://techcrunch.com/2011/04/10/peter-thiel-were-in-a-bubble-and-its-not-the-internet-its-higher-education.

Michael Ellsberg

Michael Ellsberg interviewed dozens of millionaires and billionaires for his 2011 book, *The Education of Millionaires*, revealing their self-directed strategies for success. He also blogs for Forbes, dropping punchy insights like this:

> So, how do you sidestep all that competition, the miles upon miles of jobseekers standing in employment breadlines in the same suit with the same college diploma, begging for the same job, holding in their outstretched arms—with an expectant, hopeful, yet also panicked look—their identical-seeming resumes with identical standardized credentials?
>
> It's very simple. Instead of jumping through the same hoops everyone else is suiting up from a young age to [jump] through . . . you need to develop a strong—violently strong—distaste for jumping through hoops.[63]

Penelope Trunk

Author and entrepreneur Penelope Trunk writes a compelling blog packed with sound advice for young adults. Here she argues against going to graduate school as a "safe" maneuver in a recession:

> The best thing you can do for yourself is take time to figure out who you are and where you fit in the world. No one teaches you that in school. You need to do it yourself. Grad school is a

---

63 Michael Ellsberg, "Life Lessons From a Fire-Breathing, Stilt-Walking Billionaire," *Forbes*, July 22, 2011, http://www.forbes.com/sites/michaelellsberg/2011/07/22/life-lessons-from-a-fire-breathing-stilt-walking-billionaire.

way to delay this process, rather than move you forward. . . . So instead of dodging tough questions by going back to school, try being lost. It's normal, and honest, and you will end up with more self-knowledge and less debt than your grad-school counterparts, and in many cases, you will be similarly qualified for your next big job.[64]

James Altucher

Writer and financier James Altucher writes poignantly (and irreverently) against college, and, unlike many, he provides concrete alternatives:

Here's a basic assignment. Take $10,000 and get yourself to India. Check out a world completely different from our own. Do it for a year. You will meet other foreigners traveling. You will learn what poverty is. You will learn the value of how to stretch a dollar. You will often be in situations where you need to learn how to survive despite the odds being against you. If you're going to throw up you might as well do it from dysentery than from drinking too much at a frat party. You will learn a little bit more about eastern religions compared with the western religions you grew up with. You will learn you aren't the center of the universe. Knock yourself out.[65]

---

64 Penelope Trunk, "Don't Try to Dodge the Recession with Grad School," *Penelope Trunk Blog*, February 3, 2009, http://blog.penelopetrunk. com/2009/02/03/dont-try-to-dodge-the-recession-with-grad-school.

65 James Altucher, "8 Alternatives to College," *The Altucher Confidential*, January 30, 2011, http://www.jamesaltucher.com/2011/01/8-alternatives-to-college.

Chris Guillebeau

As of late 2011, Chris Guillebeau had visited 178 of the world's 193 countries. His 2010 book, *The Art of Non-Conformity*, will light the fire of any would-be blogger-writer-entrepreneur. From his website:

> Every year, a large number of young people go through the same ritual—hours upon hours spent explaining why they deserve the privilege of becoming indebted to a system that probably won't train them for a job. For many (not all, but many), the main benefit of graduate school, or even college or university in general, is a form of life avoidance: I'm not sure this is what I want, but at least I won't have to think about it for a while.[66]

Steve Jobs

The late Steve Jobs, iconic college dropout and founder of Apple, gave an incredible commencement speech at Stanford in 2005. Here's an excerpt:

> I naively chose a college [Reed] that was almost as expensive as Stanford, and all of my working-class parents' savings were being spent on my college tuition. After six months, I couldn't see the value in it. I had no idea what I wanted to do with my life

---

66 Chris Guillebeau, "An Academic Confession," *The Art of Non-Conformity*, http://chrisguillebeau.com/3x5/academic-confession. Also, don't miss Guillebeau's essay "Qualifications" on the same blog (http://chrisguillebeau. com/3x5/qualifications) and his "Skip Graduate School, Save, $32,000, Do This Instead," Powell's Books, September 28, 2010, http://www.powells. com/blog/guests/day-2-skip-graduate-school-save-32000-do-this-instead-by-chris-guillebeau.

and no idea how college was going to help me figure it out. And here I was spending all of the money my parents had saved their entire life. So I decided to drop out and trust that it would all work out OK. It was pretty scary at the time, but looking back it was one of the best decisions I ever made. The minute I dropped out I could stop taking the required classes that didn't interest me, and begin dropping in on the ones that looked interesting.

It wasn't all romantic. I didn't have a dorm room, so I slept on the floor in friends' rooms, I returned coke bottles for the 5¢ deposits to buy food with, and I would walk the 7 miles across town every Sunday night to get one good meal a week at the Hare Krishna temple. I loved it. And much of what I stumbled into by following my curiosity and intuition turned out to be priceless later on.[67]

---

67 Steve Jobs, Commencement Address, Stanford University, June 12, 2005, http://news.stanford.edu/news/2005/june15/jobs-061505.html.

Final Inspiration

Choosing to follow the ZTC path may not magically turn you into the next Steve Jobs. But it also doesn't have to end with you living in your parents' basement. Somehow, it's become assumed that dropouts are either billionaires or burnouts, and college is the only guaranteed way to achieve success.

But you don't need college to earn money.

You don't need college to lead an interesting life.

You don't need college to see the world, be independent, build skills, or find fulfillment.

To find true success, you need self-knowledge. And you can build self-knowledge a million different ways. While college is one of those ways, it is not necessarily the best—or cheapest, or most worthwhile—for you.

Whether or not you choose to attend college, you can still use the lessons in this book to begin your self-directed journey, right here and right now.

Drop me a line and let me know where you land.

—Blake
yourstruly@blakeboles.com

Acknowledgements

My first thanks go to the teenagers and staff of Not Back to School Camp, Unschool Adventures, and Deer Crossing Camp. You're the best people I've ever met, and it's for you that this book is truly written.

Self-directed learners Tara Dean, Sean Ritchey, Ben Hayes, Weezie Yancey-Siegel, Brenna McBroom, and Allen Ellis kindly shared their stories with me, adding color to an otherwise abstract ZTC strategy. (And Grace Llewellyn created the summer camp that connected me to almost all of them—thanks again, Grace.)

Jessica Barker, Brenna McBroom, Nate Singer, Matt Sanderson, David Evitt, Matt Barney, Dev Carey, Allen Ellis, Marcia Miller, Laura Carpine, Flo Gascon, Jeff Sabo, Dianne Flynn Keith, Nathen Lester, Dean Lapham, R. Brent Mattis, Claire Bangser, Robyn Westerkamp, and Cameron Lovejoy provided invaluable feedback on an early draft of the book. You guys rock.

It takes a tribe to write a book. Leah Schulson edited my manuscript with speed, precision, and insight—while simultaneously balancing a full load at Harvard. Incredible. Can I hire you to edit my life? Lori Mortimer (proofreader), Kristen Haff (cover designer), Eric Butler (interior designer), and Betsy Dean (indexer): Thank you for making this book look and feel so much better than anything I could have done myself.

I'm indebted to three specific books that ignited my journey down the Zero Tuition College path: Daniel Pink's *Drive*, Geoff Colvin's *Talent Is Overrated*, and John Taylor Gatto's *Weapons of Mass Instruction*. And I'm indebted to Jim

Wiltens for introducing me to so many of these (and other) books that have changed my life. Thanks, Jimbo.

Robyn Westerkamp and Stephanie Grubb-Franco helped me with referrals, Diane Flynn Keith provided essential marketing advice, and Cameron, Brenna, Jessica, and Aria made those epic Leadership Retreats in Ashland possible.

Dev Carey, you're pretty much the wisest person on this big blue planet. Our conversations during the 2011 Writing Retreat and your warm guidance in the years preceding pointed me in all the right directions. I look forward to more adventures together in the years ahead.

Perhaps nowhere else have I built more self-knowledge than in the California High Sierra and, more recently, the Blue Ridge Mountains of North Carolina. Wilderness is a mirror to our true selves. Thank you to all those who keep places like these clean, open, and free.

Every day I realize a bit more how lucky I was, and continue to be, to have the mother, father, siblings, and extended family that I do. Loving support is the foundation on which all self-directed learning rests.

Finally, a huge number of friends, family, acquaintances, and complete strangers helped provide the financial backing necessary to publish this book. People like you are the ones who fuel revolutions. My thanks go out to:

Alan Lamberg

Alex Oliver

Allen Ellis

Amy Carpenter-Leugs

Amy Childs

Amy Edwards

Amy Milstein

Andy Anderson

Andy Pearson

Angela McGill

Anna Brown

Annette LeMay Burke

Antonio D'souza

Anya Kamenskaya

Arne Wensch

Ashlee Bildzukewicz

Aubree Nygaard

B. Lucky

Becky Betts

Bernard Zahanek

Beth Cannon

Brad Pendergraft

Brad Williams

Brady Endres

Brandi Jones

Brian Carson

Cameron Lovejoy

Cara Barlow

Caroline Jones

Carolyn Ellis

Carsten Schmidt

Catherine Fox

Cathy Boeker

Cathy Grahame

Cheryl Etzel

Chris Westerkamp

Christel Hartkamp

Christina Norberg

Christina Pilkington

Christine Yablonski

Cid Lough

Claire Bangser

Claire Larsen

Colleen Paeff

Cora Braun

Dan Williams-Capone

Darren Beck

David Blake

Deb Kauffman

Debbie Caldwell-Miller

Debbie Eaton

Deborah A Cunefare

Deirdre Aycock

Devin Fraze

Diane Crayne Gardner

Dulcita Love

Elizabeth Winslow

Ellen Behm

Emily Hathaway

Emily Troper

Everitt Family

Flo Gascon

Frank Cicela

Gail and Broc Higgins

Gail Proto

Georgia Ainslie-Hamblin

GoodLife Homeschool Services

Heather Booth

Heather McLean

Heather Newman

Heidi Case

Heidi Hankley

Heidi Neilson

Herbert Lapham

Ivan Staley

Jacquelin Pitre

Jane Valencia

Jascha Sundaresan

Jay Davis

Jaydeep Singh

Jeffrey Trull

Jen Lynch

Jennifer Constable

Jennifer Neary

Jennifer Shearin

Jessica Gayton

Jessica Sexton

Jihjong Larson

Joanna Lodin

John Upchurch

Jonathan Dunn

Jonathan Vincent

Joshua Teusink

Josie McKee

Judyth Brown

Julie McPherson

Julie Valvano

Karen Bartlett

Karen Tucker

Karin Miller

Kate Rafter

Kathleen Bowers

Kathyann Natkie

Keegan Atkin

Keely Seals

Kelli Traaseth

Kelly Wilson

Kevin J. Browne

Kim Driscoll

Kim Eabry

Kim from California

Kim Taylor

Kimberley Wall

Kim-dog Souers

Kip Kozlowski

Kristen Feuerstein

Kristle Kugler

Krisula Moyer

KT Patrick Bothwell

Lars Morten Fuglevik

Laura Bowman

Laura Ellis

Laura Flynn Endres

Laura Honig

Laurie Nelson Alexander

Laurie Wolfrum

Leanne Primrose-Brown

Leo Edmiston-Cyr

Liang Liao

Linda Lockwood

Lisa Biesemeyer

Lisa Biskup

Lisa Cottrell-Bentley

Lisa Filion

Lisa Henderson

Lisa Idarraga

Lisa Nielsen

Lori Mortimer

Lynn Ekstedt

Marcia Miller

Margot Cooper

Maria Hines-Brigham

Marin Holmes

Mark McBroom

Mary Alice Madaris

Mary Ann Malkoff

Mary Beth Kite

Mary Gold

Mary Jamba

Matt Jones

Matt Sanderson

Melissa Kruger

Melissa Wiley

Michael Ellsberg

Michael Mottmann

Michael Rose

Michelle Wardlow

Miranda and Bill Demarest

Miriam Brougher

Mischa Holt

Moira Ramsey

Nancy Machaj

Natalia Forrest

Natalie from California

Natalie McIntire

Natalie Pond

Nicolette Downs

Nicolle Christensen

Nikki Graham

Nina Sutcliffe

Paige Breisacher

Paul Sakol

Polly Craig

Priscilla Sanstead

R Brent Mattis

Rachel Govette

Renita Keatley

Robyn Coburn

Robyn Westerkamp

Ruth Glowacki

Ryan Singer

Sally McGinty

Sandra Dodd

Sandy Kelly

Sara McGrath

Scott Bockheim

Sean Patrick O'Toole

Sean Ritchey

Shannon Loucks

Sheeva Lapeyre

Shelly from Louisiana

Shonna Morgan

Susan Gallotte

Susannah Sandow

Tammy Hoeltke

Taralei Griffin

Tom Campbell

Tracy Liebmann

Van Messer

Victoria Day

Zen Zenith

and Zsuzsanna Dianovics

INDEX

A NOTE ABOUT THE PUBLISHING OF THIS BOOK

One of my big goals for *Better Than College* was to be able to give it away to those who needed it most. In the world of traditional book publishing, that's not easy. So I opted instead to publish this book myself, keep the rights, and give it (or sell it) to whomever I pleased.

I didn't want my book to look and feel like a stereotypically "self-published" work, in which the author assumes that he must do everything himself. I assembled a team of freelance editors and designers to produce a clean and professional final product.

To pay for all this help (plus other publishing expenses), I needed startup funds. Using the website IndieGoGo.com, I created a fundraising campaign that offered special rewards (like pre-ordered, signed paperback copies of *Better Than College*) in exchange for contributions. The 33-day campaign raised $9,200—enough money to cover all of my publishing costs and pay myself a small "advance." Perhaps more importantly, I gained an initial audience that was excited to read my book.

Independently publishing *Better Than College* was almost as fun as writing it. As new technologies disrupt the book industry, self-directed learners like you and me gain new opportunities for spreading ideas. If you have an idea that you want to spread, I hope that you'll consider the independent route. I plan to write more about this new form of publishing at www.blakeboles.com.

Finally, I must thank Seth Godin for the independent publishing wisdom I garnered from his excellent blog, his "Domino Project" book experiment, and for meeting with me in New York City. Thanks Seth—you're an inspiration.

Notes

Notes

About the Author

BLAKE BOLES is an author, entrepreneur, and educator. He owns and operates Unschool Adventures, the travel company for self-directed teens. Blake currently lives in Asheville, North Carolina, and he travels widely. He is 29 years old.

Follow Blake at www.blakeboles.com.

Photo: Bryan Derballa

Learn as if you were to live forever,
live as if you were to die tomorrow.

Made in the USA
Lexington, KY
25 March 2013